T0182581

"Yankovich focuses on enriching existing relationships—sending care packages, scheduling check-ins—rather than forming new ones, and gives tips on how to integrate friends into family and romantic circles."—*Publishers Weekly*

"A tender ode to the most significant, romantic, and essential relationships of our lives."—**Gina Rushton,** author of *The Parenthood Dilemma*

"A joyful, hopeful and considered book that will have you texting your friends in a hurry to tell them how much you appreciate them."—**Lucinda Price,** author of *All I Ever Wanted Was to Be Hot*

"Reading *Friendship First* is a healing experience for anyone who's ever interacted with people. It will have you calling up your friends to tell them you appreciate them, reaching out to those you keep meaning to catch up with, and maybe even rekindling faded connections. A compassionate and urgent take on why friendships are vital, this book will help you realize that the greatest love story of your life is probably already around you. And if it isn't, read it again!!"
—**Sable Yong,** author of *Die Hot with a Vengeance*

"After reading this uplifting book, you will never dream of ever taking your friends for granted again. Through research and moving stories that illuminate the beauty in every type of friendship, Gyan gently draws your attention to the ways that friends sustain, shape, and serve you. Our world would be a better, happier place if we nurtured our friendships according to Gyan's guidance."—**Stephanie Harrison,** author of *New Happy*

FRIEND SHIP
FIRST

**From New Sparks to Chosen Family,
How Our Friends Pave the Way
for Lifelong Happiness**

Gyan Yankovich

Foreword by Rachel Wilkerson Miller

THE EXPERIMENT

NEW YORK

For my friends
Every single one of them

Friendship First: *From New Sparks to Chosen Family, How Our Friends Pave the Way for Lifelong Happiness*
Copyright © 2024 by Gyan Yankovich
Foreword copyright © 2024 by Rachel Wilkerson Miller

Originally published in Australia as *Just Friends: On the Joy, Influence, and Power of Friendship* by Ultimo Press. First published in revised form in North America by The Experiment, LLC.

The Experiment, LLC
220 East 23rd Street, Suite 600
New York, NY 10010-4658
theexperimentpublishing.com

This book contains the opinions and ideas of its author. It is intended to provide helpful and informative material on the subjects addressed in the book. It is sold with the understanding that the author and publisher are not engaged in rendering medical, health, or any other kind of personal professional services in the book. The author and publisher specifically disclaim all responsibility for any liability, loss, or risk—personal or otherwise—that is incurred as a consequence, directly or indirectly, of the use and application of any of the contents of this book.

THE EXPERIMENT and its colophon are registered trademarks of The Experiment, LLC. Many of the designations used by manufacturers and sellers to distinguish their products are claimed as trademarks. Where those designations appear in this book and The Experiment was aware of a trademark claim, the designations have been capitalized.

The Experiment's books are available at special discounts when purchased in bulk for premiums and sales promotions as well as for fund-raising or educational use. For details, contact us at info@theexperimentpublishing.com.

Library of Congress Cataloging-in-Publication Data available upon request

ISBN 978-1-891011-82-5
Ebook ISBN 978-1-891011-83-2

Cover and text design by Beth Bugler
Author photograph by Dave Wheeler

Manufactured in the United States of America

First printing September 2024
10 9 8 7 6 5 4 3 2 1

Contents

Foreword by
Rachel Wilkerson Miller

I recently went for a walk in my neighborhood park after work. It was an idyllic late-spring evening, and everywhere I looked, I saw pairs and groups of friends bathed in magic-hour light: young women in nearly identical athleisure making plans for their next workout class; two white-haired men sitting on a bench, chatting in Polish; a recent Brooklyn transplant talking on the phone to a pal back home. There were friends lounging on blankets, pushing strollers, drinking iced coffee, and walking with dogs (a whole other category of friend!). It all looked so cozy, so easy.

And that's how friendship often appears from the outside, whether you look to popular culture, social media, or old yearbooks and photo albums. It can feel like everyone is hanging out with their ride-or-die, or taking another enviable girls' trip with their tight-knit group of five, or throwing a fabulous surprise party for the BFF who has been their number-one for the past decade. There's a conspicuous lack of conflict, jealousy, simmering annoyance, petty exclusions, and the kind of loneliness that can still exist when you're surrounded by other people—an absence of any sort of work.

In reality, though, forging and maintaining these ties isn't as effortless as it appears from the outside. I think we all know this, on some level, but it can be hard to remember when you're the one worried that you don't have enough friends, or that all the friends you do have secretly hate you.

Making and keeping friends takes work. It just does! That was true when I wrote *The Art of Showing Up* in 2020, and it's just as true now. What has changed in the years since then is that people are even more comfortable talking about—and being vulnerable about—the work of friendship. It's a welcome change, as I firmly believe that obscuring the effort we make in life—whether we're talking about our career ambitions, putting together an outfit, or planning meals for the week—does everyone a disservice, and pushes us all further away from one another (which is the last thing we need). And what good is effortlessness anyway? Of course these relationships shouldn't feel like a toxic slog, but, as Gyan writes in *Friendship First*, some of the most difficult friendships are the ones "shrouded in ambivalence." As someone who prefers earnestness and directness to irony and chilly detachment, I couldn't agree more. I love rolling up my sleeves and doing that good, worth-it kind of work. My guess is that, if you're reading this book, then you do, too.

We all have the ability to be part of beautiful, affirming friendships, whether they last for a summer, a decade, or a lifetime. This book, written by someone I couldn't be prouder to call a friend, is a great place to start.

RACHEL WILKERSON MILLER is the author of *The Art of Showing Up: How to Be There for Yourself and Your People* and *Dot Journaling—A Practical Guide*, and she's the editor in chief of SELF magazine. Her writing has appeared in *The New York Times*, VICE, and BuzzFeed, and she's been a guest on NPR, the *Today* show, and *Good Morning America*.

Author's Note

For the most part, I have used people's real names throughout this book. However, due to the personal and deeply intimate nature of our friendships, especially those that come to an unexpected end, some names have been changed throughout as indicated with an asterisk.

Introduction

"All anybody wants is to be outside and to be with friends," I huffed into my phone, watching small groups of two or three gather, distanced, on the grass. In 2020, when our worlds became infinitely smaller in a matter of weeks, I remember walking along New York City's West Side Highway, sending a voice memo to a friend in Australia, where I am from. In that moment, I felt my own basic needs whittled down to two things: fresh air and friendship.

The world was two months into the pandemic before I saw anyone I knew, other than my partner, with whom I shared a one-bedroom apartment. Two friends were cycling upstate for the day and realized their route could take them along West 21st Street, right by our place. I woke up early, washed my hair, and put makeup on for the first time in weeks, all to wave at them out of our third-floor window. They may have been the ones getting the fresh air that day, but that injection of friendship brought me back to life.

Weeks later, in an act of pure desperation, I bought a bike of my own and cycled across the Williamsburg Bridge to Brooklyn to meet a friend. We sat, masked, on opposite sides of a six-foot white circle, which had been painted on the grass. I couldn't see her entire face, but she was there. Right there. I have a photo from that day on my phone, my friend smiling under her mask with the New York City skyline behind her. I might have assumed I would look at that photo one day and feel the sadness of that time, the isolation and loss that was happening all around us. But all I feel is happiness. Fresh air and friendship: I had been right.

By 2020, I had already spent a large portion of my career as a journalist writing about the relationships we have with ourselves and others. It didn't matter where I worked, who I wrote for, or what my job title was, I always found myself coming back to friendship. At first, it was a magazine feature I'd write in my spare time, in addition to the monthly beauty pages I'd already been assigned. But years later, friendship would become my focus for weeks then months at a time as I carved out new spaces at the websites I worked at.

Still, the pandemic signaled a turning point—not just in myself but within people around the world. By the time I started writing this book, it was as though everywhere I turned, there was a story about friendship waiting to be told.

Today, four years on from those early months of the pandemic, I've wondered if my realization about the importance of friendship was in fact an inevitable conclusion that I would have eventually reached, one way or another. Virus or not, there are turning points in all our lives that open our eyes to the people who are there to hold us in moments of crisis, whether from a distance or up close.

Eventually, I would like to think we would all have found the value in caretaking and efforts to maintain relationships with people who are isolated. Because regardless of what's going on around us, our friendships, much like the air we breathe, are necessary for our survival. It just takes some of us a little longer to realize.

And for those who are yet to understand, I hope this book can be a catalyst.

~~

The pandemic created a microcosm in which the importance of friendship became clear. It was this global event that encouraged many of us to look back on our histories, and forward to the future, and see the powerful impact friends can have on our lives. Connection, after all, is a human need, necessary for our well-being.

A 2005 study titled "Effect of social networks on 10-year survival in very old Australians: The Australian longitudinal study of aging"[1] looked at the friendships of older Australians living in care facilities. After ten years, researchers found that people with large networks of friends lived longer than those without, even if they had social connections with children and other relatives. Even when demographic, health, and lifestyle variables were controlled, it was clear a decade later that friendship was fueling survival. A 2018 study,[2] which took place in China, found that breast cancer patients with close social and emotional ties in the six months following their diagnosis had both better survival rates and fewer recurrences of cancer in the following three years. Most surprising to researchers was the finding that physical well-being was less important than friendships when it came to the future of their patients.

But despite everything we know about the impact of loneliness on our well-being, and the emotional-caretaking roles friends often play in times of ill health, we live in a society that doesn't seem to understand friendship as a matter of life or death. There is no leave policy that allows us to take time off work to care for someone outside our own family who needs us. In the US, there are no federal laws that require workplaces to offer bereavement and compassionate leave to employees, and states that do offer this kind of leave generally only do so in the event of a family member's death. Many of the rules under which we live consistently ignore the facts.

When considering what we lose when we stop valuing our friendships, our minds may wander to sadness, isolation, and even moments of helplessness. The reality is that as we grow older, and all work for longer, the connections we rely on for survival become more important than ever.

Working on a story about friendship for an international news outlet, I interviewed a woman named Sylvia, who was eighty-seven at the time. She told me about her group of friends, all of whom she'd met sixty years earlier when she moved to a new street in the suburbs. While she was the only one in the group still living on the street, the rest of her friends having downsized or moved into retirement communities, she still sees all the women regularly. At the end of our phone call, Sylvia gave me a piece of parting advice I've held closely ever since.

"As I say to my granddaughters, at your age, collect a lot of friends. You don't have to be close friends, but acquaintances, because when you get to my age and people start falling away, it can become quite lonely," she said.

It was Sylvia's mention of acquaintances that stood out to me most. There is value to be found in all kinds of friendships, from our deepest and most life-affirming relationships to relatively casual connections. I'm lucky to still have friends from childhood, whom I hold on to dearly, thankful for our shared history. But I also know and appreciate the joy of new friendships—some of which I hope to nurture until they evolve into old friendships, and others that I appreciate for the fact that they are fleeting.

It is terribly clichéd to say that strangers are just friends you haven't met yet, but when I think of Sylvia and her group of friends, I'm so thankful someone knocked on her door when she moved to that street or that she waved from her front lawn to theirs. Regardless of how those women came together, there was a single moment that turned two strangers into acquaintances, who turned into friends who have stayed together for the rest of their lives. I'm constantly reminded that most clichés have their foundations set in truth.

~๑~

When I think about my life so far, a montage of moments shared with my friends drifts before my eyes.

I can see myself walking home from school with a best friend, stopping halfway to sit on the grass by the creek. I remember that same friend sitting across from me on a park bench outside our high school art class and coming out; then, in a flash I see him years later, dancing beside me in the crush of a music festival dance floor. I can feel the warmth of a friend's blond eight-week-old daughter, whom I met just hours after finding out another friend had lost her son. I remember the way her lightness buoyed me in my grief. I am huddled in a walk-in closet with my coworkers, taking turns to cry, after we found out we could all be losing our jobs. I hear myself weeks later, telling a bartender that my friend and I had got new jobs and, for the very first time, not balking at the sight of a restaurant bill.

What I find most interesting about the memories I share with my friends is the many versions of myself I see within them. While the sets and characters in these memories have remained the same throughout the years, the flashes I see of myself are sometimes unrecognizable. Like the soundtrack to a film, my friends are the chorus behind the crescendos that have signaled every moment of growing up and succeeding, of healing and of changing. My friends have always been there, vital and necessary. Together, they are the only people who could build a complete mosaic of my adult life. The best parts and the very worst—together, they're the ones who know me best.

There are many feelings specific to friendship. There's the way a friend's name can bounce around your head as you wait for them to reply to a text, when you think they might be mad at you. The ache the morning after a former friend appears in your dreams, even though you haven't spoken in years. The pang of seeing two friends hanging out without you. The emotional whiplash of seeing a friend fall in love with the right person, while another falls in love with the wrong one. The painful shock of a friend doing something you never thought they'd do to you. The regret of doing something to a friend that you never thought yourself capable of. The hurt of being told, in an email of all things, that somebody doesn't want to be your friend anymore. The shame of finding out someone needed you the day you forgot to reply to their text. The disappointment of canceled plans, the warmth of long phone conversations, or of being introduced as someone's friend for the first time.

While it would take more than a lifetime to read every romance novel, listen to every love song, or sit with every

piece of art made for a lover, the books, films, and music
dedicated to celebrating friendship are limited. Without the
same diversity of literature and cultural touchstones, how
are we supposed to understand friendship as deeply as we
do romance or family? When you take the time to sit closely
with friendship, it's surprising what's still left to uncover.

So this isn't a book about lovers, parents, siblings, or children. It's just a book about friends. It's a book about the way
friendships can be both a rock-hard wedge and a cushion of
comfort in the relationships we have with others. It is about
the way our friends can hold us when those bonds fall apart.
Above all else, it's about the friendships themselves, and how
they can become the most important and influential relationships we have in our lives.

Regardless of how much each of us believes we already
understand about friendship, there are always more steps to
be taken, more depth to explore. By learning about other people's friendships and delving into these relationships, we will
be able to reflect on our own friends, their roles in our lives
and society, now and into the future. I hope these chapters
open your eyes, mind, and heart as much as they have mine.

1

Meet Cute

One of my favorite things to do in public places is try to spot friends meeting each other. Two people furiously waving at one another from opposite sides of a busy road, waiting for the signal. At a restaurant, a man's eyes glancing up from his phone before widening, his whole face breaking into a smile, as he sees a friend pushing open the heavy door. In Washington Square Park, a pair of teenage girls hurtling toward each other with such gusto that they almost fall over with the swing of their backpacks. Every day, if you're looking for it, it's easy to bear witness to friendship. What's not so easy to see are the intricacies that exist within each of these relationships.

Having written about friendship for close to a decade,
I've used the word "friend" more than most people. I've
spoken to my friends about their friends. I've talked to people about the friends they wish they had. My friends. Your
friends. Our friends. For someone so obsessed with a single
word and all that it represents, I can understand why it may
be assumed I also have a single definition for what it really
means to be a friend. But the truth is, it's complicated. For
some of the people I have interviewed, a true friend is someone to plan a life alongside, be vulnerable with, and provide
for. To others I've spoken to, a meaningful friendship has
existed without even exchanging names. Dictionary definitions point to words like "trust," "bond," and "affection,"
as if those words aren't equally open to interpretation. It's
difficult to talk about friendship in the way it truly deserves
without more precise language to do so. For all the words
we have to describe the varying stages of dating or falling in
and out of love—whether you're seeing each other, taking
things slow, exclusive, engaged, married, on a break, broken
up, separated, or divorced—we are short-changed when it
comes to language about friendship. Despite our collective
obsession with inventing new words and phrases to describe
the way romantic relationships unfold—from ghosting
to breadcrumbing to love-bombing—friendship has been
largely neglected. While I believe the magic of each type
of friendship is impossible to perfectly capture in words, I
also understand our desire for labels, which are, as the writer
Sable Yong stated,[1] how we tell the sugar from the salt.

I'm not the first person to reflect on our lack of language around friendship. In their coauthored memoir *Big Friendship*,[2] Aminatou Sow and Ann Friedman present their own definition for the most "affirming— and most complicated— relationships that a human life can hold." To them, the label "big friendship" has come to replace terms like "best friend" and the somewhat infantilizing "BFF," which they believe don't do justice to the emotional work they have put into their relationships. For readers of their book, and former listeners of their podcast *Call Your Girlfriend*, "big friendship" is a useful label for the relationships they spend their lives tending to. But if "big friendship" sits at one end of the scale and complete strangers dangling their feet off the other, what labels, nicknames, and words dot the space between? In romantic love, the gap between so-called "soulmates" and "just friends" is stuffed with labels that describe everything from "friends with benefits" to "high school sweethearts" to "holiday flings." To leave the space between best friend and near strangers as sparse as we do—save for vague and unimaginative terms like "good friends" and "acquaintances"—is to ignore the complexity of all friendships, whether they be big or small.

In her book *The Art of Showing Up: How to Be There for Yourself and Your People*,[3] Rachel Wilkerson Miller, who I'm lucky enough to call a friend, defines a specific kind of friendship she calls the "deep-shallow" companion. According to Rachel, this kind of connection is "the height of intimacy demonstrated through extremely not-intimate conversational topics" and essentially exists through chatting daily about anything and everything. She believes that everyone would benefit from having one friend to fill this role.

When I think of this kind of relationship, my friend Gina comes to mind. Almost every day, she and I talk, text, or voice message about "deep" topics like work, our health, and our relationships, along with "shallow" topics like what our leftovers taste like the next day or whether we should wear skirts more often. While it would be strange to contact most of my friends about the minutiae of my life, I message Gina without a second thought, knowing she'll appreciate it because I feel the same whenever I hear from her.

As Rachel explains in *The Art of Showing Up*, a lot of loneliness can stem from not having a deep-shallow friend. As we grow out of high school, college, and shared apartments, then often out of jobs that allow us both the physical space and idle time to chit-chat all day with our colleagues, deep-shallow friendship can become more of an effort to maintain. And, like anything in our lives, the more effort something takes, the less likely we're able to convince ourselves to do it.

I've thought a lot about the shared experience of catching up with a friend after an extended time apart and feeling as if nothing has changed. In my experience, this phenomenon is most likely to occur with a friend you have spent a significant amount of time in deep-shallow communication with. I think of friends I've lived with, swapping stories of our days each evening; of friends I worked retail with, doing laps of the shop floor in twelve-dollar ballet flats that made our feet ache; and of friends I would spend all day at school with, only to go home and ask my mother if I could call them on our home phone. The years I spent with them have left these friendships comfortable and familiar, like a well-worn sweater, no matter how long it's been between wearings.

Whatever terms we use, invent, or still lack, those of us who are lucky enough to have experienced friendship of any kind know it when we feel it. And while there is something incredibly fun about applying a sticky label to a friendship and bringing new language into our collective lexicon, the sheer depth and breadth of all possible types of friendship means it would be impossible to define each and every one. So perhaps, instead of focusing on our lack of friendship labels, it's worth considering the limits labels place on the relationships we have with our families and romantic partners. Maybe part of understanding the complexity and vastness of friendship is accepting that some relationships are impossible to put words to.

The joy of casual friends

When we talk about friendships to admire and aspire to replicate, it's all too easy to get swept up in the lore of perfect best friends, life-changing connections, and relationships that last from childhood into old age. As much as I love to celebrate these friendships, I also believe that many of us are consistently overlooking the value to be found elsewhere, in the friendships that exist somewhere in the middle of the road. I'm talking about the friends we speak to once a year, the ones who exist at the center of a very specific Venn diagram where two separate social circles overlap, the ones you're always happy to run into at a party but would never text afterward. I'm speaking of our low-stakes acquaintances and the friends who only exist to you in one particular place, whether it be in a nail salon, workplace, café, or lecture hall.

A 2014 study, "Social interactions and well-being: The surprising power of weak ties,"[4] found that weak ties, like those we have with acquaintances, improve our social and emotional well-being. Essentially, this research found that the more we interact with people on a daily basis, even when these people aren't close—or even good—friends, the happier we are. While close friendships can take years to come into their own, there's comfort to be found in the tiny friendships that exist at the periphery of our daily lives.

Unlike close friendship, where it's easy to see the impact you have on one another's lives, another unexpected joy of casual friendships can be the difference you make in someone's life without even realizing it. A 2020 report from Settlement Services International[5] shared findings of researchers who spoke to 334 refugees with permanent residency in Australia. One of their primary findings was that most of the refugees interviewed reported high levels of trust in their neighbors, despite communication difficulties due to language barriers. Rather than bonding over suburban gossip, these small and trusted friendships were built from simple everyday encounters, like a wave, a smile, or a hello in passing. There is so much value in offering warmth in small doses, even if we're not sure a relationship will ever grow into something more.

When I think of all the people in my life I could call a friend, it's almost overwhelming how wide this definition can stretch. From some of the most meaningful and long-term relationships in my life to people I sat across from in an office years ago, the ability to see how every kind of friend can impact your life is an important one. Reframing our idea of what it means to be someone's friend is the first step in bearing witness to friendship in all its forms and, hopefully, feeling less alone.

What we really mean, when we say we want new friends

In 2019, I wrote an advice column answering the question of a reader who was scared they may never make new adult friends. They were in their twenties and, despite making some friends at university, found that most of these people lived quite far away. On a deadline, but deeply invested in the anonymous stranger on the other end of the internet, I paused over every word in the letter. The writer opened with a wish for "new, interesting, loving, and honest" friends, before stating their desire to have friends close by to meet for dinner and drinks. The desire to find people who are interesting, genuine, and filled with love is not too high a bar to set. In fact, it's what we should all strive for. But what I saw in the letter were two different wishes, both equally valid, but also possibly best solved by very different relationships.

At the time of writing my reply, I was living and working in New York, a city where having a social life revolves around bars, restaurants, gigs, shows, and the people you go to them with. When I arrived in the city in 2017, sitting closely behind my goals of "find an apartment" and "work out what a credit score is" was my intention to find people to hang out with. Most of my closest friends were in Sydney, existing in an opposite time zone, and they remained the people I reached out to when I was feeling anxious or had good news to share. If I had moved to the US with the intention of finding new friends to replace my closest circle, I would have been setting myself up to fail.

Answering this letter, I thought about the different friends I had and the needs we all met for each other. While there is comfort in relying on a close friendship, having someone to catch up with for a drink once a month can be just as beneficial. Thinking of the letter writer, I worried that there were kind, genuine, loving people in their life that they were discounting as friends because they lived too far away to catch up for walks, brunches, and drinks. To close yourself to friendship, whether it be long-distance or extremely low-stakes, because it doesn't meet all your expectations is to potentially miss out on something really special.

If you've decided you want, or need, to make new friends, I'm of the belief that the first question you should ask yourself is: What do you want from a friend? Do you want someone to work out with or go to the movies with or text all day? Do you want someone to eat lunch with once a week or someone to call when your parents are unwell and you need a ride to the airport? Do you want company or someone who shares a certain interest your other friends do not? While it's impossible to truly predict how a friendship will unfold—part of the joy of new friendships is their ability to surprise us, unfurling in unexpected ways—this understanding can help guide our approach to meeting new people. The understanding that it's rare to find one friend who fulfills all your expectations and wants is the key to opening yourself to the many kinds of friendships that can exist.

In the years I've been writing about friendship, both before this advice column and far beyond it, one question has always been louder and more consistently repeated than the rest: How do I make new friends? If you start where I recommend you do when it comes to friend making and ask what kind of friend you want to make, it's a logical next step to consider where exactly this person might be. Unfortunately, the answer to this very practical question isn't quite as straightforward.

The time and patterns of friend making

If you crunch the numbers cited in a 2018 research article titled "How many hours does it take to make a friend?"[6]— which tells us it takes thirty hours to make a casual friend,

140 hours to make a good one, and more than 300 to make a best friend—it's no wonder none of us feels like we have time to cultivate new friendships. Factor in the time we spend with family, dating, working, running errands, plus undertaking an estimated twenty-one hours of extra unpaid labor every week if you're a woman,[7] and you have a pretty depressing state of affairs. Even if you're not spending your few free hours each day exercising, watching TV, or refreshing the same three apps on your phone, the stranger-to-friend investment time-line borders on oppressive. But what do these numbers really show us? To me, they demonstrate why we're most likely to make friends with people we spend time with at work, where we're contractually obligated to orbit each other in proximity for a designated number of hours per day. It can feel simple, bordering on reductive, to tell people to look for new friends wherever they spend the most time, but if my calculations are correct, it's also a promising place to start.

Of course, work isn't the only place to meet new people. A friend of mine once told me about someone she became close with after striking up a conversation in the line for the bathroom, after one of them pointed out they were the only two women in the nightclub wearing sneakers. I know two women who crossed paths while both traveling solo and now plan a vacation together once a year. My own partner set me up on a friend date with someone he was chatting with while waiting for a visa appointment at the US consulate. Part of the magic of falling in love—whether it be romantic or platonic—is not knowing exactly when it will take place.

But like the frustrating cliché "it will happen when you least expect it," the advice to "look for new friends everywhere" isn't particularly helpful or reassuring.

Whenever I've tried to find patterns in friend making, outside of work and overlapping routines, the other common factor that emerges is life transitions. When I reflect on going to university, leaving my hometown, starting new jobs, moving overseas and moving back again, I remember how open I was to meeting people and going out of my way to connect with them during those periods. I'd like to think I'm consistently open to new friendships, but when I think back on these seasons of change, I can acknowledge the blinkers that are likely shielding my eyes from the potential of new friendships whenever my life is more stagnant or I'm more comfortable sitting in my place. It's during those periods of great change, inspired by anything from heartbreak to migration to gender transition, that we can crack ourselves open and see who sneaks into our lives before we settle and gently close ourselves, like a clam that's drawn in enough oxygen from the surrounding water and is ready to shuffle back into the sand.

However, the timing of life transitions and our desire for new friendships don't always coincide with those of others. Early in my career, still new in Sydney, I assumed that everyone who worked in my team would soon become a friend of mine outside work. But that's not what happened at all. Many of the people starting at the magazine where I worked had friendship groups outside work, partners, families, or long commutes out of the city that meant they weren't free for after-work catch-ups like I was. I'm sure some of them simply didn't like me as much as I liked them. What I eventually learned was that making friends in a new city was akin to a very slow-moving game of Tetris in which I was constantly having to bump up against brick walls until eventually I found a space in a friend-ship group where I fit. Sometimes I was the first piece to hit the group, welcoming friends to fill the space around me until we became a solid unit. Other times, I tried desperately to fit myself into someone's world, only to find that no matter how charming, funny, or generous I tried to be, they weren't inter-ested in fitting new people into their life.

In the years that have followed that life transition, during which I first became obsessed by the art of friendship, I've been surprised by how often friends can be found by look-ing back and around, not just forward. I've reconnected with people I used to work with, only to become closer than we ever were when we shared an office. I've made friends with my friends' friends, and jump-started friendships with people who had sat in the periphery of my world for years. When we talk about making friends, emphasis so often falls on the "new," as if the only way to build a connection with someone is to start completely from scratch.

When I interviewed Kristen S. He, a trans writer living in Melbourne, Australia, about her friendships, I went into the conversation expecting it to focus on the people she had welcomed into her life since transitioning. And while we spoke in-depth of friends she has made who helped guide her journey, she also reflected on the old friends she has connected with in new ways since transitioning and how those relationships have changed for the better.

Kristen went to an all-boys Christian high school and, despite having many issues with the school's philosophy, classism, and approach to masculinity, she's stayed connected to a group of friends from childhood who are all straight, cis men. When they started using her name and pronouns correctly after she came out, she felt a shift. The group may not have been new, technically, but she was a new version of herself and so were these friendships. "We were rewriting twenty-five years of history, in some cases. Together we'd all come to an understanding about my life, and it wasn't just a superficial thing, it was actually quite a deep acknowledgment of who I am," she told me. "I found that to be really beautiful."

As we enter new chapters of our lives and begin to feel different from the people we were in the one that came before it, finding new friends who only know this version of ourselves can feel like a tidy solution. But if we really want to open ourselves up to friendships in new ways, looking back on the people we may want to revive a relationship with can be just as good a use of time.

Wave first, make an effort

A 2023 study titled "The surprise of reaching out: Appreciated more than we think"[8] found that we consistently underestimate how much people in our wider social circles appreciate being reached out to "just because" or "just to catch up" through text, email, or a phone call. In my own experience, the sentiment rings true. At any given time, I have a running list of old friends in my head who I know I should message but don't out of fear that they won't want to hear from me or are too busy with other friends to catch up. Still, I can't recall a time when I've ever heard from an old friend and wished I hadn't.

In *Mindwise: How We Understand What Others Think, Believe, Feel, and Want*,[9] psychologist Nicholas Epley writes that "nobody waves, but almost everybody waves back." This idea, that most of us have difficulty being the person to make the first move, whether it be in dating or in our friendships, is also linked to what's known as the "liking gap." When I interviewed Dr. Marisa G. Franco, author of *Platonic: How the Science of Attachment Can Help You Make—and Keep—Friends*,[10] for a feature about making new friends in person, that phenomenon is one of the first things that comes up in our conversation. "When strangers interact, they tend to overestimate their likelihood of being rejected. And the more self-critical you are, the more pronounced your liking gap is," she said.

To combat the liking gap, Dr. Franco encourages people to always assume others like them, calling on another phenomenon known as the "acceptance prophecy."[11] This concept suggests that the way we interact with people can become a self-fulfilling prophecy. When we assume people don't like us or don't want to become friends—as the liking gap encourages us to do—we come across as reserved and cold. But when we walk into a group or conversation assuming that we are liked—that people want to become friends with us—we enter it with warmth. I don't have to try very hard to imagine myself in either scenario. I'm too familiar with the instinct to cross my arms, the desire to reach for my phone and lean out of a conversation, or the assumption that silence is the only way to avoid embarrassment when listening to a group's inside joke. On the other hand, I also know the feeling of meeting someone and having no doubt that they're grateful to be getting to know me. That feeling is one of life's greatest joys.

The emotions we project onto our potential friends have big consequences. A research article titled "Empathy and well-being correlate with centrality in different social networks"[12] studied college dorm students during their first year on campus and found that people's individual traits directly matched the kind of friend they became to others. Students who were consistently positive became the friends people looked to for fun and excitement, while students who were known to be empathetic became the people who were sought out for support and trust. Allowing other people's perception of you to change the way you act around them may seem calculated, but when you consider it a prompt to let your best qualities, whether they be positivity or empathy, attract new friends, this kind of introspection has tangible benefits. If having people come to you with their problems makes you feel needed and helpful, it's important to let people know that you care about them. And if you want to be invited to parties or have a packed social calendar, it helps to show people how much fun you are to be around. So long as you're not faking it, showing people the best parts of yourself is an easy way to attract friends who see you the way you want to be seen.

When I reflect on the periods of my life when I was most desperate to make friends, I feel proud of the way I moved past the belief that I was fundamentally shy (it turns out I'm not), stretched out of my comfort zone, and clung to the hope that eventually I'd find my people. But at the time, like many people looking to make friends, my desires were shrouded with feelings of shame.

"Have you made any friends yet?" is the question most asked by parents of their kids after they've started school, but it's also one I've been asked after moving, going to university, and in the first months of a new job. Often, it's been one of the hardest questions to answer at objectively difficult times. Because the truth is, meeting new people and finding community isn't necessarily easier than finding somewhere to live or work. In fact, these things are often more connected than we might imagine.

So what's holding us back?

While the liking gap and our approach to reaching out to people are theoretically individual choices, and we can all work to improve our chances of making friends, there are also systemic reasons for why it can feel so impossible to make new friends right now.

In his 1989 book *The Great Good Place*,[13] urban sociologist Ray Oldenburg first presented the idea of the "third place." According to Oldenburg, third places are those conducive to socializing that exist outside our homes and workplaces, such as parks, cafés, churches, and public libraries, where there is little financial barrier to entry. In TV shows, particularly those that center around a friendship group, the third place is usually obvious—the Central Perk coffee shop in *Friends* being one of the best-known examples—and serves as a backdrop for a substantial number of scenes in each episode. But in reality, third places can be much harder to find.

For many people, it's not just a lack of free time holding them back from socializing with others. It's also a lack of disposable income. The rising cost of eating out, joining clubs, and attending events limits people's access to third places and, in turn, their interactions with new people. Even for people on a livable salary, expenses around socializing are often the first to be cut when you're trying to spend less. Dinner with a relatively new friend can be hard to justify when you have upcoming plans with old friends or family that are going to cost you, whether it's buying a birthday gift for your niece or traveling for a wedding. Meeting new people can already feel like an emotional risk, but when you're tight on money and time, it won't always feel like a risk worth taking. And when finances within a friendship change, as the cost of living continues to rise and wages in many industries stagnate, dynamics can quickly shift. Continually pulling out of plans because of their cost, without an affordable option to suggest in their place, isn't exactly helpful when building a friendship.

Ideally, third places would be plentiful and either low-cost or completely free. But again, getting access to places like this—even the free ones—can be more difficult if you're in a lower tax bracket or a certain minority group. A 2020 report by Conservation Science Partners[14] found that "low-income, underrepresented, and minority communities"—including Black, Hispanic, and Asian American groups—were more likely to live in nature-deprived areas. Neighborhoods with a lot of greenery—whether it be a park, public garden, or sporting field—are often highly desirable, which pushes prices up, and pushes people who can't compete financially out and into areas without these things. Less affluent suburbs are often crowded with houses or apartment buildings, meaning there are even more people competing for a place in already limited green spaces in addition to other community facilities, like libraries. Giving up easy access to parks as a third place becomes the trade-off for more affordable rent or mortgage repayments.

As depressing as it feels to draw direct links between the cost of living and our ability to cultivate new friendships, it can serve as a helpful reminder that making friends can be difficult for many reasons—some of which we can change and others that we can't. As long as the unfairness and injustice of inequality touches everything from people's health and homes to their friendships, it's important to be gentle with ourselves when considering the barriers to friendship and to recognize that while there's much we're incapable of changing (at least in the short term), acknowledging difficulty is often a first step to overcoming it.

2

The Friendship Recipe

Visiting New York on one of the last warm days of fall, I met my friend Isaac in a Brooklyn bar with another friend, VJ, whom I hadn't seen since I left the city two years earlier. We each had plans that night, so we dove in right away, desperate to squeeze as much juice from our two-hour catch-up window as we could before going our separate ways. At the time, Isaac was in the final stages of planning his wedding, and as we cycled through everyone who would be attending, I felt close to my friend as we remembered times I'd spent getting to know the people in his life outside our own friendship groups, from his soon-to-be wife's parents to friends who left the city not long after I arrived. After years of friendship, which have involved Isaac bringing friends together, whether at a dive bar playing pool or being cooked for in his apartment, I've come to know many of the people he holds close.

I've known Isaac since we were teenagers, but this familiarity with his friends and family can't be explained away by decades of crossing paths. Each introduction, party, dinner where Isaac has casually invited an extra friend along has—whether he's realized it or not—brought the people in his life closer. And when someone shows that they're trying to connect the dots between the friendships in their life, it's so easy to want to do the same. Now, friends of mine who have never met Isaac know him by name.

I looked at Isaac across the table, just a glass of Prosecco and two cheap beers between us, and asked how he got so good at bringing the people in his life together. How is he such a good friend?

"Am I?" he replied.

I looked back at my friend—this friend who has helped me move (more than once), dropped sourdough starter at my door during the pandemic, and, on this very trip, found me a place to stay after I left my job and wasn't sure I could afford to come anymore—and I had to stifle a laugh. It's funny to me that being a good friend can come so naturally to someone who doesn't seem to understand just how valued their efforts are.

What comes so easy to Isaac can feel impossible to others. When I think of my own approach to friendship, I fall somewhere in between. I find it easy to talk to new people, but I also find comfort in shrinking away as soon as I feel everyone else in a group is funnier or more interesting than I am. I plan myself a birthday celebration each year, but every single morning, on the day of the event, I always regret my decision, anxious that nobody's going to have a good time. People don't necessarily gravitate toward me, but they do hover close enough for me to reach out and grab them by the elbow when I'm feeling up to it.

There are a million different ways to show a friend you care, but when I think of Isaac, and other friends who show their love in different ways, the common denominator is always action. If you really want something, you've got to work for it.

I've often found that within my friendships it's the small and unexpected gestures of kindness I remember most. A friend surprising me with a lunch of their leftovers, someone remembering the names of my colleagues or how old my nephew is turning this year. No matter the friendship—however big or small, long or short—nothing worthwhile comes without some degree of effort.

Friendship fuel and flexibility

In 2019, Julie Beck began a project for *The Atlantic* called The Friendship Files. Over three years, she conducted 100 interviews about friendships, then published a story on every single one. At the conclusion of the series, Beck wrote about the recurring themes she witnessed through these conversations: accumulation, attention, intention, ritual, imagination, and grace.

Beck calls these themes the "forces that fuel friendship."[1] In this final piece, Beck writes of the time that is needed to build a friendship (accumulation); the effort it takes to recognize when there's a potential friend to be made (attention); the action required to take that step toward friendship (intention); the importance of shared routines, habits, and traditions (ritual); the ability to see friendship as capable of more than casual companionship (imagination); and love and adoration (grace). If there were a recipe for friendship, I think this would be it.

The older I get, the more I enjoy cooking. I will marinate, roast, simmer, and pan-fry. Baking on the other hand, is not for me. While cooking is an art, where improvisation and experimentation are encouraged, baking is a science. If I were to compare the recipe for friendship to either culinary exploit, the flexibility it requires makes it—much like cooking—an art above all else.

When I speak to Beck over the phone, flexibility quickly comes up in conversation. "Friendship can be anything. And friendships can be anything," she tells me. By this, Beck refers to the fact that while the very definition of friend is flexible, so is the list of feelings and favors that contribute to a friendship's being real in the first place. But while there is no checklist of gestures that you can work through to certify your friendship,

Beck believes that the ability to be flexible with your friendships and the people sitting at the center of them is key. After all, a good cook knows how to make a recipe their own.

"My one piece of advice is to reach out to your friends more than once," she says. "We have a turn-based idea of how we schedule socializing in our very calendar-oriented society. People are like, 'I reached out, they said they were busy, now it's their turn to reach out to me.' It's not in a mean way, necessarily, it's more like we don't want to bother anyone. But I honestly believe we're too polite to our friends. Just reach out again! People feel very grateful when someone else does the labor of setting up something social. And it takes sustained time and effort to turn somebody into a friend."

A whole host of invisible and unspoken expectations can send a friendship off track. Differing opinions on what constitutes a timely text reply, mixed definitions of what it means to "flake" versus reasonably cancel plans, and the space that exists on either side of personal boundaries, which is too often left open for misinterpretation. Everything that remains unsaid in these situations can rot and corrode friendships. Long periods of time left waiting for a friend to get in touch with us can create wide chasms in our friendships. In our romantic or family lives, we're often more comfortable demanding an explanation from a loved one. But when it comes to friendship, too many issues often remain unresolved.

Another approach to flexibility, which I believe to be just as important, is the acceptance that our friendships are ever-changing. I can admit that, in my early twenties in particular, I was a very demanding friend, a give-me-all-of-yourself-or-give-me-nothing kind of friend who couldn't ever feel close enough to those closest to me. If I had my way, which I often did at that time, I would have eaten every meal with a friend, done my weekly groceries with another, and shared a bed with anyone in my closest circle every night, falling asleep satisfied that I'd get to wake up with a friend beside me. When reciprocated, this kind of closeness is magic. But the thing about friendships with such high expectations, and such little flexibility, is that they can easily break. In my first shared apartment, I practically chased my roommate halfway into the city one day after feeling incredibly hurt that she'd left for work that morning without me. It turned out, she'd just wanted to call her long-distance boyfriend on her walk—something I definitely didn't need to be around for.

As I've grown older and been able to reflect on how much I needed from my friends at that time, I've become more comfortable with the ebb and flow of friendships. One of the most stressful moments in a friendship can be the realization that you're not as close to someone as you once were, coming second only to the decision to end a friendship entirely. The sooner we all realize that even the best friendships come in seasons, the sooner we can watch these relationships come and go in waves, without automatically assuming a friendship has come to an end for good. While it takes confidence to start a new friendship, insecurity can become its demise.

This knowledge, as my friend Haley Nahman writes in her newsletter *Maybe Baby*,[2] can also be helpful when we're feeling envious of the friends and friendship groups of others. Interrogating her own anxiety around friendships, Haley came to realize that both friendships and groups are always in some state of flux. "They adapt, fade, restart, break apart, grow, change again. Even super solid, made-for-life type friendships go through different eras, including lulls," she writes. "Sometimes a group you assumed would be solid forever feels less cohesive because one pivotal person becomes less invested in getting everyone together. Other times you meet a new friend and they introduce you to some of their friends and suddenly you have a whole new group you regularly spend time with."

Overcoming the mental block of assuming everyone but you has a solid friendship group, or a best friend who will always be there, is difficult, particularly for those of us who have spent decades consuming pop culture that has tried to convince us that this is the norm. In reality, most friendships are constantly changing shape, either growing deeper and stronger, or shifting and creating space for new or lower-stakes friendships to thrive.

Finding (and encouraging) connection

In late 2022, writer Chelsea Fagan tweeted,[3] "Truly nothing makes me happier in life than introducing people who I just know are gonna hit it off as friends. We're having a party in a couple weeks and I will measure its success by how many new-friend hangouts emerge from the evening." This view of friendship, that connecting others is as important as being connected, is something I'm always working on. When you have people in your life whom you love, it can be easy to feel possessive of them, out of fear of how that friendship could change with new people brought into the mix. But accepting that a friendship can still exist even when group dynamics change or new people come into the fold feels like unlocking a new level of trust and intimacy.

This concept is one that Priya Parker discusses in depth in her book *The Art of Gathering: How We Meet and Why It Matters*.[4] When it comes to hosting gatherings, like Fagan's party, Parker agrees that a good way to gauge the success of an event with friends is by judging how connected people feel when it comes to an end. "One measure of a successful gathering is that it starts off with a higher number of host–guest connections than guest–guest connections and ends with those tallies reversed, far in the guest–guest favor," she writes.

If connection is the goal when it comes to new friend-ships—whether they're between you and someone else or within a group—it's impossible to ignite a spark without set-ting the intention to do so. To choose the right dinner recipe, you need to know what kind of meal you're in the mood for, then follow the instructions carefully. To make a new friend, you must set your sights on someone, then work to build a relationship from scratch. And just like cooking, it can take a few tries to get it right.

The effort required to make a new friendship spark, then stick, doesn't always come naturally—a realization that can feel counterintuitive to everything we know about the importance of these relationships. It can feel easy to wonder why something so vital is so famously difficult to obtain.

All friendships require care, intention, and effort. Regardless of the capacity in which friendships exist, they all involve listening, sharing, helping, advocating, and loving. Even our most casual relationships don't happen by accident. It could sound transactional to suggest people should consider what they can offer their friends, while thinking about what their friends offer them, but I also see this as a way of acknowledging—at least to ourselves—the give and take, push and pull, a close connection requires.

Both vulnerability and action are key ingredients of the friendship recipe. Even the act of identifying someone as a friend requires overcoming a kind of humility—a trust in them to refer to you as the same. To be able to properly discuss friendship, it's vital to know the different shapes these relationships can take, the care they require, the difficulties that surround them, and the ways in which we must all work to tend to them properly.

There's a certain kind of satisfaction I can only find after a delicious meal. A joyous kind of fullness. One of the only feelings I can compare to the sensation is in the hours after spending time with one of my closest friends. Driving back to my place from a friend's or lying in bed after a late night at a bar, I swear I can feel a deep hum inside my bones, as if I've spent hours plugged into a glowing electric socket, then returned home recharged. To me, this feeling is what makes the difficulty of making friends worth it. It's why I'm happy to spend time asking myself what I can offer people, then making sure I do. It's why I think about who I want to become closer with, then edge myself, inch by inch, into their lives.

The recipe for friendship has many ingredients. Of these, some will be the secret sauce, touching everything each relationship involves, while others will be a garnish, making a certain connection feel special when compared to others. By understanding that there are many elements that help a friendship form, no matter how big or small it is, we can better understand what it takes to become and to stay someone's friend. Because these realizations are important, especially as we look to challenge the worldview that friendship must always sit in second place, behind other kinds of love.

3

Family Matters

The first time I told my friend Tim I loved him we were both fifteen.

Tim and I had met in elementary school, and he was the only boy I invited to my sixth birthday party. It was a dress-up affair, and Tim, true to form, came dressed as a "person"—a fact we still laugh about today because, despite all that has changed in the decades we've been friends, Tim's disdain for costume parties has not wavered.

The following year, I changed schools and didn't see Tim until summer vacation five years later. Outside our local supermarket, our moms spotted each other and stopped for one of those mom-to-mom chats every preteen dreads. After quickly working out that we lived on opposite sides of one of our town's main roads, my mom suggested that Tim and I walk to and from school together. Now eleven, memories of my sixth birthday party long faded, I couldn't believe she was doing this to me. After we parted ways and stepped onto the escalator to leave the shopping center, out of earshot from Tim and his mom, I hissed at mine for embarrassing me. I didn't want to be friends with *whoever that was*, thank you very much. After being placed in many of the same classes, Tim and I eventually came around on my mom's suggestion and spent most afternoons after school walking home together. We played compilation pop albums out of Tim's portable CD player, we'd sit by the creek that flowed under a rickety wooden bridge (a path I was strictly forbidden from taking, unless I was walking with Tim), and then often finish our walks home with a visit to one of our houses for a glass of water after spending thirty minutes in the beating sun. By the final two years of school, despite being in different friendship circles, we were incredibly close.

Tim and I were both growing up in public housing with single parents, so when our Ancient History class planned a trip to Pompeii it wasn't exactly a surprise that neither of us was able to go. On the weekend most of our classmates were overseas, we decided the only suitable substitute for the trip would be to spend the night locked in my bedroom watching *The Lizzie McGuire Movie*, which is famously set in Italy. We watched the film, took photos together to upload to Myspace, and at the end of the night my mom asked if Tim wanted to stay over. Once again, I was embarrassed by her suggestion. Tim was a friend, sure, but he was still a boy, and in my teenage mind, that placed him in a different category from my girlfriends, whom I always wanted to invite for sleepovers.

In hindsight, this was one of the first signifiers that Tim and the friendship we had was special. By the time Tim came out to me one afternoon on a park bench outside our art class, there was no other way I could have responded than with, "I love you."

Many scenes from the early years of my friendship with Tim could be given a sepia treatment and not feel out of place in an indie coming-of-age film. But when I remember that time, I don't just see the burgeoning friendship of two teenagers, I see a connection that existed outside class, or even school, and held space within my family. When I was elected as the female school captain, my mom's excitement for me was equal to her disappointment that Tim wasn't going to be my male counterpart—since he was elected vice captain, meaning we often weren't paired together on projects or at assemblies. When Tim returned from four months of backpacking in Europe a week early to surprise his friends and family, he turned up at my house to find I wasn't there; Mum called me and, not wanting to spoil the surprise, simply told me to get home *immediately* with a sense of urgency I couldn't imagine her using for anything other than a true emergency. I was in such a rush to get there I reversed into a utility pole while pulling out of a parking lot and crumpled in the back of my beloved 1993 Suzuki Swift.

In those years, and still today, I considered Tim family—a compliment reserved only for our closest friends. But why? Family matters for many different reasons, but one of the most ignored is the influence these relationships can have on the way we value our friends.

As families change, so do friendships

In 2017, psychologist William J. Chopik undertook a study[1] with 271,053 adults, from teenagers to people in their seventies, from ninety-seven different countries. While a lot of research had already proved the effect that close relationships have on our overall health and well-being throughout our lives, Chopik wanted to compare the effects of different kinds of close relationships. Namely, he wanted to look at family, spouses, children, and friends.

Chopik's research found that people who place a higher importance on friendships have "particularly better health, happiness, and subjective well-being at older ages" than people who don't. More specifically, the research found that for people in older adulthood, the positive effects of friendships are stronger than that of their familial relationships. The study also found that the more important people's friends are to them, the more likely they are to feel the benefits of having these close relationships.

To me, one of the most interesting things about a study that compares the relationships we have with our parents, siblings, partners, and children to those we have with our friends is that there's no guarantee people will have all—or even any—of those meaningful familial relationships. And when we look at the family sizes and structures of generations before us, we know millennials are statistically less likely to have as many children or siblings as our parents or grandparents. In 1910, the average American household was made up of 4.54 people. In 1959, it was made up of 3.34 people. And by 2002, there was an average of 2.56 people in every household.[2] But if families are becoming statistically smaller, who exactly is filling the gaps? Our friends.

Despite not being one myself, I've always found myself drawn to only children. Tim is an only child, as is my partner, Michael. It's not uncommon for me to gravitate toward a new friend only to find out after a few conversations that they don't have any siblings—in fact, I'm quite used to it by now. I adore both Tim and Michael for a million very different reasons, but what I admire most in both is the care with which they treat their friends. When I speak to them about what it was like growing up without siblings, as I often do, their stories are very different (Tim played Monopoly alone, moving the different pieces around the board himself, while Michael spent hours in his backyard throwing a football as high as he could in the air) but the sentiment behind them is the same: No matter what you're doing, a friend can make all the difference.

The only children in my life don't fit any of the stereotypes that once plagued kids who grew up without siblings. I know that Michael and my sibling-less friends know how to share and be patient and put others before themselves because I have witnessed it firsthand repeatedly. Living closely alongside them, I have seen the way only children hold their friends close, because they know what it means to be alone. While I know the guarantees that come along with my sister's love—that I will always have someone to call, someone who can cherish my childhood as much as I do, and someone who will one day share the responsibility for our parents—I also know how it feels to fill that role in the life of someone without siblings. And it's a privilege.

One of the reasons modern households are becoming smaller is because people are having fewer children. According to data from the Centers for Disease Control and Prevention, the national birth rate in the US fell by almost 23 percent between 2007 and 2022. And while this decline shows that many people are remaining childless or child-free, the numbers also suggest that only children are becoming more common.

There's a lot of talk about what shrinking households—and populations—mean for a society. From elderly people who are without kin to care for them to the politics of an aging workforce, many discussions are being had worldwide about the impacts of people choosing to have smaller families. But little of this discussion looks at the roles friends play in the lives of those with small or nonexistent families.

I'm endlessly interested in the ways our families and friendships collide, the way they push and pull, like ocean tides. A 2015 study titled "Family and friends: Which types of personal relationships go together in a network?"[3] looked to

investigate what influence familial relationships and friendships had on one another. Researchers wanted to know: Does
having a smaller family usually mean having more friends?

The study confirmed, as researchers expected, that people
with numerous family members who have active involvement
in their life had fewer nonfamily members—like friends,
neighbors, and colleagues—in their close network. The study
also found that those without as many active family members
in their network welcomed more friends into their lives to
fill the space. What was most interesting about this research
was its focus on "active" family members. For a family member to hold their place in someone's social network, and not
have their role filled by a friend, they needed to actively par-
ticipate in the relationship. The study found, essentially, that
even if you do have siblings, parents, and other relatives, they
still need to consistently show up if they want to remain part
of your life. People want to feel that they have a network they
can depend on. So people who don't have dependable family
instinctively look to bring their friends closer.

When your biological family is small, friends become more
than an insurance policy—they become a lifeline. Since I was
a child, I've had friends who have little to no recollection of
ever meeting one of their parents, despite their being—as far
as we knew—alive and well. At school, I had friends with parents who were incarcerated or living so far away they were
unable to be part of their kids' day-to-day lives. By the time
I turned thirty, I had a handful of friends who had already
lost a parent, some while they were teenagers and others in

the decade following. I've sat with friends after they've spent afternoons in hospitals and held them after funerals. But just as prevalent as loss is the need for care.

Today, I have friends who are legal guardians or emergency contacts for siblings who are physically or psychologically unable to reciprocate the kind of care they are being provided. And I have friends with no interest in reconnecting with their siblings or parents for a variety of reasons, ranging from clashing personalities to abuse. As positive a person as I aim to be, I'm not delusional enough to think that this trend of unwell parents, broken family ties, and sibling tensions won't continue as my friends and I enter middle age and beyond. Life, after all, only becomes more complicated. While some of us are fortunate enough to maintain faith in the promise that our family will always be there for us, the reality is that this isn't always the case. To assume that everyone has a biological family who can care for them unconditionally is to discount the experiences of people who were separated from their parents, who have family members living with addiction, who were unable to have children, or who have been rejected by the family they were born into. The reality is that when it comes to family, there are no guarantees.

Who are we? And who understands us?

In *Far from the Tree: A Dozen Kinds of Love*,[4] Andrew Solomon presents the idea of horizontal and vertical identities.

According to Solomon, vertical identities are those that are passed down to children through DNA and shared cultural norms. These include ethnicity, eye and skin color, language, and, for some, religion. Horizontal identities, on the other hand, are those that are foreign to someone's biological parents. Solomon spoke to hundreds of people with shared horizontal identities and their families, including those diagnosed with deafness, autism, and Down syndrome, as well as people who have committed serious crimes despite being brought up by parents who haven't, child prodigies, and trans people with cisgender parents. In the book, and in the world around us, there are endless examples proving that horizontal identities can provide bonds just as strong as, or even stronger than, vertical identities.

"Modern life is lonely in many ways, but the ability of everyone with access to a computer to find like-minded people has meant that no one need be excluded from social kinship," writes Solomon. "Vertical families are famously breaking down in divorce, but horizontal ones are proliferating. If you can figure out who you are, you can find other people who are the same."

While the "horizontal identities" Solomon explores so deeply in his book are big, weighty, and, in most instances, life-changing or -defining, the existence of the term prompts me to think of the tiny horizontal identities we can each carry. For example, being vegan, loving video games, playing a certain sport, or being a fan of a particular band are tiny horizontal identities that don't necessarily separate us from our biological families in a meaningful way but can spark connection to a new community of people with shared interests and experiences. And there are even smaller things too, not always substantial enough to be classed as an identity, that can leave us feeling more connected to our friends rather than to our family.

But horizontal identities need not operate at the expense of our vertical identities. Soon after turning sixty, my mom joined a local motorcycle club, where, on weekends, she rides her vintage BMW, which she had stopped riding when pregnant with me. My sister became a mother years before I'd even thought about my own fertility, and I see how she's bonded with friends who were raising babies at the same time she was. When I hear my family mention friends I haven't met, I don't feel distant from their lives. I'm happy that they've found people they feel close to, who can offer them things that I can't.

The more people there are who can understand us in ways our family can't, the less pressure there is on our families to know every part of us. When we take a different path from family, for whatever reason, friends can lift the expectation that the people we're related to by blood should know us better than anyone else.

Many millennials are part of what's known as a "sandwich generation," defined by the Pew Research Center[5] as a generation of adults with at least one living parent sixty-five or older also raising a child younger than eighteen or providing financial support to an adult child. Essentially, a sandwich generation is made up of people who are juggling the care of two other generations—the one above and the one below. A friend recently spoke of how it felt to be caring for her toddler while also caring for her elderly parents, one of whom was dying of cancer. It's a scenario you wouldn't wish on your worst enemy, but it's one that a lot of us will face. If you're lucky enough to have loving parents who live a long life and to have children, if you want them, it seems the trade-off is the space in between, when you inevitably—particularly if you're a woman—become a caregiver for all.

As society is currently structured, caring roles for our young and old often fall to our biological family. But what of the care needs of the caretaker? Who is there to mind the children while the caretaker's parents are being taken grocery shopping? Who stocks the fridge of someone who has spent the week driving between their kids' school pickup and parents' doctor appointments? Even the sandwiched adults with healthy parents and healthy children are left to carry the emotional labor that can come alongside love, care, and obligation. For people squeezed into the center of the sandwich generation, friends can be a welcome release for the pressure. Relatability is at the heart of most friendships. We're drawn to people who *just get us* and whom we understand in return. In adulthood and middle age, connection that was once found by bonding over assistant-level jobs with deplorable salaries and badly behaved housemates is found in new ways. Friends who are of similar age to us are the people most likely to understand the squeeze of the sandwich generation, arriving to give support at a time when empathy and advice can be far more valuable than a proposed solution to an unsolvable problem.

Blurring the lines between friends and family

Almost every summer of high school, I would spend two weeks with my friend Bess's family. They vacationed in the same spot, a campsite hidden between a beach and a sloping national park. Even now, it's one of my favorite places in the world. When I first started going camping, Bess and I were typical teenage girls. We were moody with her parents and slept in late every morning until the tent got too hot to bear, when we could emerge and throw our duvet-wrapped selves onto a beach lounge to continue dozing. Everything we wore that first summer was hot pink, and the inside of our tent was filled with hot pink bags we'd collected at the mall. I still remember, clear as day, Bess telling some local boys we met on the beach that she'd be sixteen next year—a fact that was technically true, even though she was fourteen (while I was still thirteen) at the time.

Bess's family, much like her, are loud, clever, kind, and a little eccentric. For the first few years, I felt nervous when her aunties pulled me in for tight hugs or her cousins asked me about school or my plans for college. The intimacy of two weeks spent with a family who were so eager to welcome me felt intimidating. But as years passed and Bess and I grew older and closer, it no longer felt like I was being invited along on *their* camping trip; it felt like my summer tradition too.

Without the blessing of school vacations or the freedom of college schedules, it's hard to spend more than a day or two at the campsite now. Still, I visit every year I can, only to be greeted by a family who will, at any cost, try to convince me to stay for lunch, stay for one more afternoon swim, stay for dinner, then stay the night in a tent that's coincidentally empty and can be *made up with a bed in just a few minutes, no hassle at all.* Alongside the identities that define us and the life stages we find ourselves in, our personalities also play a big part in the way we approach friendship and relationships with our family. A 2022 study, "Interdependencies between family and friends in daily life: Personality differences and associations with affective well-being across the lifespan,"[6] looked at the so-called big five personality traits—extroversion, agreeableness, openness, conscientiousness, and neuroticism—and how they relate to the way we interact with both family and friends.

This study found that while most people were in daily contact with their family more often than with their friends, participants were happier when with their friends than they were with family—particularly when it came to people with higher extroversion. It also looked at how our personality influences whether we are more likely to feel closer to our family network or to our friends. People who were conscientious—and thereby more sensitive in nature—tended to have more contact with their family, due to a higher sense of duty. Meanwhile, people who identified as being more open-minded, extroverted, or agreeable tended to gravitate more toward their friends, especially the latter group who often found that many people wanted to be friends with *them*.

Interestingly, researchers behind the study also pointed out that despite some family members *feeling* like friends and some friends *feeling* like family, most people still associate family with "hierarchy rather than equality" and "obligation rather than choice."

People were more likely to feel like they were volunteering their time to friends, whereas time spent with family felt tied up with a sense of duty. Even for extroverted people like me, who are most likely to have strong bonds with both their family and their friends—presumably because they have the energy to balance both—the results feel exactly right. Who we are, what life stage we're in, and what we enjoy all blur the lines of importance between our family members and friends. The one constant, no matter who sits at the heart of this conversation, is that there are endless ways friends can complement, supplement, and coexist with our families. One should never be more important than the other by default.

4

It Takes a Village

When Beau Kassas, a health worker in his thirties, met his best friend, Marie, they were at the same school in their small, rural hometown. They were also both "straight." It wasn't until Beau reached his early twenties and moved to the city that he came out, with Marie eventually following suit, coming out at the same time as another friend of Beau's, Sarah. Ten years later, Sarah and Marie are engaged and parents to a perfect little girl, Maisie.

As a gay man, Beau tells me it's not uncommon to have straight women you meet on nightclub dance floors tell you they'll have your babies whenever you want them. In fact, I remember my own friends making similar (platonic) love-fueled promises to gay men, years before anyone involved knew what being a surrogate or donating their eggs or sperm truly involved on a physical or emotional level. But eventually, if you really want a family, these conversations need to stop being drunken promises and become a reality.

When Marie and Sarah decided they were ready to start a family, they went straight to Beau. "Being Lebanese, family is really important to me. I didn't want to create my family with multiple mothers," says Beau. "I didn't want to donate or have a baby for the sake of it. I wanted to create a family *with family*." Having been friends for decades, Marie knew all of this about Beau. So when the topic was first broached with him, it was with the proposal that together, through IVF, he and Marie would create a number of embryos—some for Marie and Sarah, and if it all worked out, some for Beau to use when he was ready. These future babies would be biological brothers and sisters, connected as a big family with two loving moms and a dad. "If I look back on it, what I really wanted out of this type of agreement was that we would raise these families together," Beau tells me. "I'm not going to be Uncle Beau. I'm Bo-Bo or Dad. It's important for Maisie to know she has two moms but also an understanding of who I am."

Couples opting for a known donor or surrogate—rather than one found through a family planning agency, fertility clinic, or sperm donation program—are encouraged to go through rounds of counseling sessions with all involved parties to ensure that everyone's on the same page about the future. Bringing a baby into the world is a leap of faith most people don't take with their friends, but when I ask Beau how each of these therapy sessions transpired, he points out that true friendship, like the one he has with Sarah and Marie, is based on honesty and transparency. Having difficult conversations was a practice they were already used to, even if they'd never been in this exact scenario before. While Sarah and Marie still live rurally, Beau now lives on the coast with his partner, whom he met after these conversations took place. It's a lot to juggle, he admits. Sarah and Marie are Maisie's moms and full-time caregivers, but Beau tries to visit them (or vice versa) at least once a month. He struggles with not being there 100 percent of the time but understands they're still working on finding the right balance of visits and daily FaceTime calls, even after Maisie's first birthday. There are a lot of kinks to work out, but isn't that the case with every family?

If they're lucky, conception can be relatively straightforward for heterosexual couples. They're also not beholden to the same mandatory counseling that Beau, Marie, and Sarah were. I have straight friends who have amicably broken up before their toddler's second birthday and others who parent from different countries. Shit happens, especially when it comes to families. I ask Beau how he feels about undergoing a level of interrogation that hetero couples don't need to adhere to, simply because his relationship with Marie is a friendship and not romantic. I can already hear skeptical voices asking what would happen if Beau quarreled with his friends, or if Sarah and Marie separated. Beau has thought about it too.

"Some of that really came out in therapy because anything could happen to a relationship long term," he says. "Friendships break down, relationships break down— but that could also happen in a heterosexual relationship. Parents break up and they work out how to share custody."

When it comes to family structures, Beau says his Lebanese heritage has helped him understand that family is a cast of many. He's always been part of a big family, where all older males are "uncle" and older women are "auntie."

"We're going back to more than two people raising a child. Maisie has my parents, Sarah's parents, Marie's parents, and recently met my partner's parents, who absolutely adore her— she has four sets of grandparents instead of just two," he says. The idea that a community of people raising Maisie and her potential future siblings could be anything other than a blessing just doesn't make sense to Beau, given his own cultural definitions of family. In his ideal world, all parents would have close groups of friends who are raising their children side by side whether they're related or not. "Friendships can move toward family with time. When you trust friends the way you trust your family, you can have it all."

When Beau mentions trust, I think of the many expectations I have within my closest friendships. I trust that secrets will be kept, judgment will be withheld, and that there will always be a place for me in their lives, so long as I keep up my side of that same bargain. And while friends can let you down on any number of these things, so too can family. In fact, for many people I know, it would be far more shocking for a friend to drop the ball on these desires than a parent.

The more I have thought about friendship, the more blurred the lines between "how to build a friendship" and "how to build a family" have become in my mind. Both relationships require love, duty, patience, trust, and tradition. The point at which family often diverts onto its own course is when the topic of children arises. But as I come to understand the ways family and friends can build, connect, and grow together, the more I'm sure that the future of the family will evolve to include friendships sooner than some people might expect. For families like Beau's, that future is already here.

Rethinking the definition of family

Who gets to call themselves a family? For some, this feels like an easy question to answer. A family is made up of parents and children. A family is stable. A family stays close because its bonds are clearly defined and often bound by blood, marriage, or other legal documents. But if you're able to dig a little deeper, it becomes clear that the nuclear family has never been the only kind of family that makes sense—nor is it exactly working out. In a feature for *The Atlantic*, David Brooks writes that "the family structure we've held up as the cultural ideal for the past half century has been a catastrophe for many."[1] Before the nuclear family became the norm in the Western world in the 1920s, most people lived in "big, sprawling households" with their extended family. According to Brooks, by 1960, 77.5 percent of American children were living in a household with their two married parents, separate from their extended family. It's easy to visualize the nuclear family ideal because it's dominated our TV screens in shows like *Bewitched* and *The Brady Bunch*. Even *The Simpsons* portrays the classic nuclear family, delivered with a hint of satire.

There are obvious reasons the nuclear family hasn't been the ideal it was once portrayed to be: women were relegated to the home; a fear of divorce meant many people stayed in unsafe or unstable relationships; and extended families were no longer cared for in the way they were in times of more communal living. Friends were also pushed firmly into second place—a position they still haven't managed to escape. Marxists believe the nuclear family benefits capitalism, promoting intergenerational inequality and maintaining class divides through family inheritance.

The nuclear family was sold on the promise of security. But as Minna Salami, author of *Sensuous Knowledge: A Black Feminist Approach for Everyone*, wrote in an essay for CNN,[2] "we are at a point in time when we urgently need to redefine and separate the notion of family from patriarchy and heteronormativity if it is to survive. Only then can we make informed decisions about what an ideal family really is."

But what's the alternative to the nuclear family? Many families today are slightly tweaked versions of the old ideal:

foster and adoptive families, families with queer parents at the helm, single parents, and child-free couples. And most of these families still function despite the age-old truth: It takes a village.

According to a 2022 research paper, "It takes a village to raise a child: Understanding and expanding the concept of the 'village,'"[3] the well-known phrase originates in an African proverb. Villagers, in this instance, are made up not only of extended family but of other community members, including teachers, neighbors, and family friends.

In a 1989 interview with *Time*,[4] Toni Morrison famously said that two parents can't raise a child any more than one. "You need a whole community—everybody—to raise a child," she told the magazine.

For anyone who has experienced alternative definitions of family—whether for cultural or personal reasons—Morrison's puzzlement as to why so much of the world is still holding on to the notion that families need to be tight-knit, private, or related by blood is one I share. Even the way many young people live today—first sharing a home with their parents, then moving into a shared space with friends or a place alone, with the perceived end goal of ending up in our own "family home"—limits the possibilities of joyful cohabitation. If we could do away with the societal assumption that families had to be nuclear, that the village could exist in reality, not just as an overused and appropriated phrase, what would people really want, deep down? I have often joked with friends that maybe, one day, we should all move onto one property with our partners and future children and live cult-style (without the actual cult stuff). But what if it weren't just a joke? What if you could build your village? How would that even work?

The history of the "chosen family"

One of the best ways to imagine the possibilities of the future is to examine the past. When I speak to Hannah McElhinney, author of *Rainbow History Class: Your Guide Through Queer and Trans History,*[5] it's 9 AM and her eyelids are bright pink. It's WorldPride in Sydney, and the night before we meet she attended a cowboy–cowgirl themed *eleganza extravaganza*, only to wake up and realize her makeup had stained her eyelids before she needed to do a live interview on morning TV. The only solution, she quickly realized, was to reapply the hot pink eyeshadow. "I think I'll just have to keep my makeup like this all Pride," she tells me before we get into it.

The term "chosen family" has become shorthand for any close friend group. In reality, the term, along with "found family," represents something a lot more complex, with deep historical roots for queer and trans communities.

While anthropologist Kath Weston uses the term "chosen family" in her 1991 book *Families We Choose: Lesbians, Gays, Kinship,*[6] the concept behind the term predates the book by decades. "Up until the twentieth century, if you were queer—or camp, as you might have been called then—you were essentially living a double life," says Hannah. "Toward the mid- to late twentieth century, coming out became more of a facet of queer life. There was the beginnings of a movement and queer activism, but this was really when people started being rejected by their blood families, pushing them to find love and acceptance elsewhere."

Beyond parental approval, in decades like the 1950s, queer women and gender-nonconforming people were also looking for ways to survive without a husband during the era of the nuclear family. "If you wanted to live with a female partner, you literally didn't have an income, so you needed other people who were also in your queer circle to provide for you," Hannah tells me. "That's how we got lesbian potluck culture, which was led by Black, Jewish, and immigrant lesbian communities working to provide for each other."

The thing about queer chosen families is that they all look a little different. In the US, the closest thing to a nuclear family for some queer, trans, and gender-nonconforming people has been found within the New York Ballroom scene, a queer subculture where most participants belong to "houses" governed by a house mother or house father. In the 2018 TV series *Pose*, the character Pray Tell, played by Billy Porter, puts it perfectly when he says: "A house is much more than a home. It's family. And every family needs a mother who is affirming, caring, loyal, and inspiring."[7]

These houses, beyond providing familial care and shelter, also organize Ballroom events. As Marlon Bailey, author of *Butch Queens Up in Pumps*,[8] has written, "Houses and balls are two core social dimensions of Ballroom culture that are inextricably linked; typically, there are no houses without balls and there are no balls without houses. Ballroom communities are transient and hold balls at different places; the transformation of spaces for balls is linked to the kinship and supportive structures that Ballroom members produce and enjoy."[9] When it comes to replicating traditional familial structures, those who belong to the Ballroom scene have figured out a way to either broaden their own family or fill in the gaps left by their own biological kin. For many, Ballroom provides a homely space and a new kinship structure, but it's far from the only example of how integral chosen family has been to the survival of the queer community in the past.

It would be both impossible and ignorant to discuss the history of the queer chosen family without reflecting on the HIV/AIDS crisis. When talking about the differences between friends and family, the phrase "blood is thicker than water" is a go-to for anyone who believes the roles that biological family plays in our lives cannot be replicated. As I talk to Hannah about the roles of chosen family, friends, and community through the AIDS epidemic, the phrase comes to mind again, but not for the reasons one might usually expect.

"In the seventies there were increasing freedoms for queer and transgender people, but AIDS just knocked that flat. There were so many people who would find out they were HIV-positive, which was then a death sentence, and have their parents and families reject them," says Hannah. "These people needed to be cared for as they died." The practice of cooking and caring for chosen family within the community was not new at this point, but the crisis brought about new ways for chosen family members to support one another: blood.

A failed cancer drug, azidothymidine, known as AZT, became the first treatment for AIDS in 1984. For many people, use of the drug required frequent blood transfusions, with severe anemia a side effect of the treatment. By the time the drug was formally approved for use by the Food and Drug Administration (FDA), it was estimated[10] that as many as three hundred thousand extra units of blood would be needed to meet the demand of patients who were taking AZT. In the early 1980s, many countries banned men and some trans people who have sex with partners who have been designated male at birth from donating blood. Lesbian blood drives[11] became a solution to the shortage, as queer women who were able to donate stepped up to help those in their community. Suddenly, the role of a chosen family was not only about acceptance, care, and love—it was about showing up, sharing blood, and surviving.

When looking back on queer and trans history, it can be easy to focus on how far community activism has taken us and how much society's wider acceptance of queer and trans people has evolved. The traditional nuclear family unit of two married parents with children might now be possible for queer people in the US, but it's still not an easy path.

And as some hurdles within the community are overcome, new ones that still need to be navigated are given space to move to the front, including those having to do with biological family. The relationship some queer people, especially second- and third-generation Australians, have with their families can get even more complicated when it includes important links to culture and religion. When what you inherit from your biological kin makes up so much of your identity, it can seem unfair to feel pressed to abandon them for the sake of another part of yourself.

"I think there's always going to be the need for queer chosen families, for that connection with queerness. Because you do have to navigate so much," says Hannah. In the hour that we talk, I notice that there are three words Hannah repeats: safety, sustenance, and care. Before our conversation, I would likely have connected these words with the act of mothering, thinking first of my own mother and then of the mother I hope to be one day. But as I listen, read, dig, and reassess, I find more and more confirmation that there are many ways to provide our friends with the love that mainstream society may have us believe can only come from a biological parent. Friends can tend to us when we're unwell, forgive us for our most shameful mistakes, and teach us new things every day.

There are many ways to be a family, and it feels like a great shame that some are considered more significant than others.

Traditions worth keeping

I love meeting my friends' parents and siblings. I also love hearing about their family traditions: games played on long car trips, birthday breakfasts, and films that are watched whenever everyone's under the same roof. But there's also a certain melancholy I have felt in the past when hearing about the sweet habits some families have, which comes from knowing it's too late to play a role within them or replicate them with my own parents. The concept of tradition plays an important part in our lives, ranging from events and rituals with cultural significance to smaller and arguably more special secret languages and routines that exist only within small family units. Traditions, whether cultural or personal, are what make family members feel connected to one another. Still, I've often wondered, why can't the same rule be as meaningful when applied to friendships?

Since 2012, Mahir Mahbub has had an annual tradition with his friends. Every December, the group of nine get together for a Secret Santa gift exchange. When it started, the limit for gifts was fifty dollars, but as everyone grew up and their salaries increased, the limit was raised to one hundred dollars. When I speak to Mahir about his tradition he jokes that one day the limit will be five hundred dollars, thanks to inflation.

Everyone in the group's parents emigrated to Australia from Bangladesh at a similar time, settling in the suburbs of Sydney. By some strange chance everyone in the group has older sisters around the same age who are also friends, and, over time, the group grew close after going to the same schools and university. As Mahir puts it, the group is a big family. "We'd all been friends for years but didn't have many traditions around the holidays. None of us are religious, despite all being raised in Islamic households," Mahir tells me. So one Tuesday every December, the group gathers for their annual gift exchange. Ironically, as celebrating Christmas is haram (forbidden by Islamic law), they meet at a halal steakhouse for all-you-can-eat ribs and wings.

When Mahir looks to the future he sees his friendships and their traditions colliding with his biological family. "We don't want the tradition to stop," he tells me. "We'll probably get our kids in on it in the future." For many people, Mahir included, the best traditions are deeply connected to their family or their family's culture. However, for others, the art of building new traditions around friendships is a reminder that you don't need a close family to have future rituals to cherish and look forward to.

What draws most of us toward family is the promise of unconditional love. That promise is why I know deep inside my chest that my parents would be there for me, no matter what. It's why I'd do just about anything for my sister or my niece and nephews. But while family can contain our most precious connections, they should never be the *only* ones we resolve to put effort into.

And while I would hope never to detract from the love and connection so many people find within their family units, it's vitally important to acknowledge this experience is not available to everyone. Friendship, on the other hand, is. Growing up without holiday and birthday traditions doesn't mean you won't ever be able to celebrate them. Favorite meals, cooked after difficult days, don't have to come from the kitchen of a grandparent—they can just as easily come from a friend.

To say that a friendship can never be as meaningful as a bond we have with a sibling or parent is to tell people who don't have those ties that the love they receive from even their closest friends will always be second-rate. As proven by different cultures and communities for hundreds and thousands of years, the bonds we form with those who aren't bound to us by romantic love or blood can be all those things and so much more.

The unexpected power of obligation

When it comes to friendship, we're often drawn to people with interests, values, and experiences similar to our own. My single friends have other single friends; friends who are training for marathons spend hours every weekend with other friends who are also interested in running marathons. The same logic can be applied to a myriad of other scenarios too though: friends who have lost and longed for the same future, friends who have lived experience with the same kinds of discrimination, friends who might not share blood but share culture.

In her book, *Sisterhood Heals: The Transformative Power of Healing in Community*,[12] Dr. Joy Harden Bradford writes about the concept of collectivism in the lives of African Americans, particularly Black women. The idea of collectivism is closely tied to "obligation," a word I have always previously associated with biological family. "Collectivism refers to the tendency to put the needs of others in the group before your own," writes Bradford. "This tendency often shows up in the sense of obligation many have to community uplift, to leave something better than we found it, and to ensuring the longevity of our community."

As the founder of Therapy for Black Girls, an online space dedicated to the wellness of Black women and girls, Bradford is vocal about the fictive kinship between Black women, even if when they're not related by blood. "It's this collectivist sensibility," she writes, "that creates an expansive notion of what it means to be a 'sister' to someone within this community."

After putting the very concept under a microscope, I wonder: If we all loosened our grip on what it means to be and to have a "family," would people in my life still be working to maintain relationships with their biological kin who have mistreated them? Would I have more friends who have children without a romantic partner, if the fear of raising them alone were erased? If we could trust that our friendships were enough to keep us safe, secure, and cared for, who would we really want around? And if we accept that our friends can love us just as much as our family can, how big could our communities grow, blending family and friends, with love as the ultimate adhesive?

5

The Care Factor

A few years ago, I wrote an essay[1] featuring a somewhat unconventional piece of life advice: Always offer to help your friends move.

Moving is widely considered one of the testing tasks of any relationship, as you put your knees, back, and patience on the line to get everything you own from one location to another in a matter of hours. In 2019, despite having lived in the US for less than two years at that point, I somehow managed to have a completely full apartment, packed with clothes to suit the extremes of every New York season, and as much furniture as we could squeeze into our square footage. So when my partner and I made plans to move to a new neighborhood, I insisted we call in the professionals—this was, somehow, a job way too big for two. My plan would have gone ahead if it weren't for our friend Isaac, who insisted we save the money and let him help us pack and haul our belongings from one side of Lower Manhattan to the other.

In New York, much like any other major city, it's easy to catch up with friends. There are countless new restaurants and shows and parks to walk laps on a sunny morning. There are places to meet for coffee and art exhibitions everyone tells you are must-see. What's less easy to do with a friend is commit to a plan that can't be canceled. And what's more uncancelable than a move?

While I had a large enough circle of friends in the city at the time with whom I could easily have made plans to grab a drink, I had just a couple who offered their help and company during the move. These were friends I would offer the same help to, friends who weren't just looking for company in a new city but a safety net too.

The more un-fun things I do with a friend, the closer to them I feel.

The day before our official move, my friend Jess piled into an Uber with me and a carload of my belongings, balancing a box of pots and pans on her lap. Jess was the first guest in our new apartment, one of the only people to see its completely bare walls until my partner and I moved out years later and a different friend, Erin, cleared out our final belongings while we were already on a plane halfway back to Australia. When Erin was finished, she slid the brass-colored key I carried with me for two years under the apartment's front door, closing that chapter of my life for good.

My logic about helping friends move also explains why we're more likely to make a friend at work while packing up chairs together after an event than we are at the event itself. It explains why I'll always remember the day Bess and I dug trenches for an irrigation system on her property, but I'll never be able to tell you what we had for dinner that night or anything else we did that weekend. It makes a case for putting in the work for your people.

Looking back on my friendship-defining moments while writing that essay, it was interesting to see how few of them took place at a restaurant or a party. Moving is, inarguably, a terrible task. But helping a friend move, much like building flat-packed furniture or changing a tire with someone, is a reminder that for friendships to find depth, you can't only do fun things together. Sometimes, getting your hands dirty is the key, a reminder that true friendship is about more than the good times.

Loving, caring, doing

What does it mean to love a friend? Not just to say *I love you* with conviction, but to really, truly love a friend the way we're made to believe we can only love a sister, mother, or romantic partner?

In *All About Love: New Visions*,[2] bell hooks wrote that while the word "love" is most often used as a noun, all love would be better if the word were thought of as a verb. Love, hooks believed, is an action—something that must be performed over and over again. While we are often taught that we have no control over our feelings, we are told that actions have consequences. When love becomes a verb, it becomes something we do, something that we choose. To love, hooks wrote, is to nurture and to care.

When I think about the relationships I have with each of my friends, the unique ways we care for one another sit at the front of my mind. The friendships I have built on a personal pursuit of caregiving are those that mean the most to me. Years ago, the importance I now place on care may have come second to the importance of *fun*, when nights out, the speed with which someone could reply to a gossipy text message, and a shared desire to camp at three-day music festivals mattered more to me.

Today, those elements of frivolity and recklessness sit well behind the comfort I find in friends who not only ask how I am but consistently *know* how I am, because of the work they do to put together the pieces themselves. These are the friends who know when I'm nervous about an upcoming doctor's appointment, have a writing deadline I'm struggling to meet, or am fixating on a big decision. It's inside these friendships I find the most support, guidance, advice, and kindness—the most fertile soil in which to sow the seeds of my future. This kind of care can be the proof that someone is willing to invest as much in me as I am in them.

For a generation obsessed with the simplicity of Gary Chapman's five love languages[3]—words of affirmation, quality time, physical touch, acts of service, and gift giving—the complexity of meaningful caregiving can be its undoing.

Depending on the person and their situation, caring for someone means listening, supporting, celebrating the good days that shine through the bad, understanding on a deep level exactly why something matters to a friend, and tending to them in their most vulnerable moments. As someone prone to overthinking, I recognize that caring for me often involves my friends acknowledging the same questions (Should I buy this? Could I wear that? Is that something to be mad about or am I losing touch with reality?) repeatedly, knowing when to offer advice and when to simply sit back and listen until I tire myself out.

For other friends, many much less demanding than I am, care may take the form of errands, reading over cover letters and résumés, or committing to a night out, even when they don't feel like it.

Care will never be a simple box you can check, but that doesn't mean it doesn't belong at the top of our friendship to-do lists.

The problem with therapy-speak

After I published the essay about moving, it stayed in the back of my mind for years, until a tweet[4] went viral in early

2023. The tweet argued the opposite of my essay—and many of my beliefs about care—in two simple lines, encouraging people to hire movers and save their friendships. On a practical level, I suppose I understood it. Moving is time-consuming and physically taxing. To some people, it's a lot less stressful to cough it up and pay for professionals. On its own, the tweet wasn't particularly offensive, but it was just one part of a wider conversation that's been happening on social media for some time, one that turns away from the types of care and service I believe we should provide to our friends. It presented a sanitized version of friendship, complete with rigid boundaries and language that's now known as "therapy-speak."

The language trend, which people have adopted in the real world, in texts to their friends and on their dating profiles, relies on phrases typically used by mental health professionals. Therapy-speak has normalized people "being at capacity" and "not having the bandwidth" to deal with their friends' problems. The new course of language has, in many ways, signaled an HR-ification of regular conversation. It could also be argued that therapy-speak has led to an increasingly casual use of terms like OCD to describe someone who is really organized, rather than someone diagnosed with obsessive-compulsive disorder, and the misuse of words like "trauma" and "abuse."

In a 2021 feature for *The New Yorker*,[5] Katy Waldman posits that the language of mental health is burgeoning, because our actual collective mental health is doing the complete opposite. "We joke about our coping mechanisms, codependent relationships, and avoidant attachment styles. We practice self-care and shun 'toxic' acquaintances [. . .] We feel seen and we feel heard, or we feel unseen and we feel unheard, or we feel heard but not listened to, not actively," she writes. "Our emotional labor is grinding us down. We're doing the work. We need to do the *work*."

For many people, therapy can be lifesaving. And it can save friendships too, by helping us to better understand and communicate our feelings. The tools that psychologists, counselors, and other mental health practitioners have provided to society in recent years are invaluable. Thanks to them, we now have a toolkit of phrases, words, and affirmations to help us put words to some of the most complicated feelings there are. Still, it could be argued that when it comes to therapy-speak, it's possible that some of us are doing more harm to our relationships than good.

In late 2019, Melissa A. Fabello, PhD, a sex and relationships educator, tweeted a conversation template[6] she created as an example of how to respond to a friend when you're unable to support them. The screenshot message template read: "Hey! I'm so glad you reached out. I'm actually at capacity/helping someone else who's in crisis/dealing with some personal stuff right now, and I don't think I can hold appropriate space for you. Could we connect [later date or time] instead/Do you have someone else you could reach out to?"

While I'm sure some people—especially those who have genuine difficulties with setting boundaries—would have found the template somewhat useful, the general consensus online was that Fabello's suggestion wasn't an acceptable way to speak to a friend in need, whether you were available to support them or not. Years and countless memes later, I believe there is a link between therapy-speak like this and other conversations that tells us we should never help friends move, pick them up from the airport, or answer their calls when we "don't have the emotional resources for trauma-dumping right now." While friends are never *entitled* to your care, energy or attention, there's a balance to be found between letting people walk all over you and shutting them out completely.

Whatever form a friendship takes or the context in which it exists, there needs to be a promise made: I care *about* you and I will care *for* you. For casual friends, this care could be getting them coffee when they've had a terrible morning at work or lending them a book they want to read. It could be a text to see how their job interview went last week. But for close friends, there is no end to the kind of care that can be given and received. This is the care that can be lifesaving, friendship-defining, carrying you through the darkest night and delivering you into a day you weren't sure you'd ever see.

Tending and befriending

There's a special kind of anticipation reserved only for the close friends of expectant parents. It blends a gentle respect for their space with the knowledge that, on the list of people who will find out about a baby's entrance to the world, you're sitting pretty close to the top.

I was visiting my hometown when my friend Leda sent a message to let me and another close friend know she'd given birth. Sitting in my mom's living room, I saw the picture before I read the text: a black-and-white photo of Leda and her husband in a hospital bed, cradling a perfect, chubby-cheeked baby with rosebud lips. As I read Leda's words, a ball of lead dropped from my throat deep into my stomach. Her little boy, Marlowe, was here. But he was also gone.

Two months before Marlowe was born, Leda and her partner, Chris, got married. The wedding was a surprise to all but a few close friends who were tasked with helping it come to life and invited to be part of their bridal party. The guise for the wedding was a baby shower, held at a house with a sprawling green backyard in the mountains. When I arrived (incredibly underdressed for a wedding), Leda was in a baby blue dress with billowing sleeves, which hung loosely over her perfect round belly. After Leda's cousin, who also happens to be a celebrant, announced that we were actually at a wedding, the balloons that had decorated an arbor overlooking the valley were taken down and Leda reemerged dressed in white. When I look at photos from that day, as I often do, I think of how simple happiness can be. Joy is the opposite of misery.

Leda was thirty-nine weeks pregnant when she had placental abruption, a condition which sees the placenta separates from the uterus. By the time Leda got to the hospital, she knew that her baby was gone, even before she was told by a sonographer that there was no longer a heartbeat. When I received that text from Leda, my mom, from whom I've adopted a habit of saving anything remotely fancy from ever being used—from expensive hand soap to journals with thick buttery pages—pulled a dust-covered candle from the top shelf of her bookcase and lit it. Within hours, Leda's friends around the world were doing the same, lighting candles and wishing there was a way to turn back time.

In 2013, psychologist Susan Silk and her friend Barry Goldman wrote an opinion piece for the *Los Angeles Times* titled "How not to say the wrong thing." In it, they explained the Ring Theory,[7] their formula for caring for someone in crisis. "Draw a circle. This is the center ring. In it, put the name of the person at the center of the current trauma. For Katie's aneurysm, that's Katie," they wrote, referring to a mutual friend who had recently had a brain aneurysm. "Now draw a larger circle around the first one. In that ring put the name of the person next closest to the trauma. In the case of Katie's aneurysm, that was Katie's husband, Pat. Repeat the process as many times as you need to. In each larger ring put the next closest people. Parents and children before more distant relatives. Intimate friends in smaller rings, less intimate friends in larger ones."

The rule of the Ring Theory is to "comfort IN, dump OUT." When you are speaking to someone close to the center of the crisis, who is in a smaller ring than yours, your job is to support them. If you need comfort, you should look to someone in a ring larger than your own to provide it. Everyone in each ring has a duty, and if the formula is followed correctly, everyone can both receive and give care.

When I think of Leda, she is at the center of the circle with her husband. Their own parents are next, because Marlowe was theirs too, a missing piece inside their cocoon of immeasurable grief. The people who enveloped Leda and her family were their friends, me and countless others. While Silk and Goldman's explanation relies on the idea that it is someone's biological family who will be most impacted by a crisis, understanding who really sits within those inner rings can be much more complex. It can require careful consideration. After Leda found out that Marlowe would be stillborn, the first and only person she called was her mom. On that call, Leda asked her mom to tell one of her best friends, Jess, who then organized a group chat with the rest of the bridesmaids from the wedding. "I wanted to speak to people, but it was so overwhelming," Leda tells me. "How do you even tell someone out loud, 'I'm not going to have a live baby anymore; he died'?"

Her friends sent groceries, bought food delivery vouchers, and organized a trip for Leda and Chris to take as soon as she was discharged from hospital and well enough to travel. While they were away, Leda's friends went to their home and packed up everything from Marlowe's room, organizing storage for all of his belongings, so that Leda and her husband were spared from looking at freshly washed baby clothes and the cot that had been waiting in the corner of their bedroom. Every single day during the first week Leda was back home, a friend left a smoothie on her doorstep.

The day before Marlowe's memorial, where we gathered to listen to Bob Marley by the ocean, I messaged Leda asking what I could do to help. She assigned me a basic task: bring tissues. That morning, I went to my local pharmacy and bought as many tissues as I could carry. I arrived at the lookout with a large leather tote bag stuffed with boxes and individual tissue packets, only to find that most people had brought their own. But it was never really about the tissues. On one of the worst days of my friend's life, tissues were never going to make things feel any better. All they could do was assure Leda that if she asked, she would receive. They helped me show her that if there was anything she needed, big or small, I would do it, if she let me.

As anyone who has experienced grief will know, there is no moving on, letting go, or getting over a loss like Leda's. Instead, it's just about finding a way to get through each day. In the weeks and months after losing Marlowe, Leda's friends played the biggest role in her survival. "My family were supportive, but my friends were proactive," she tells me. "My family were in shock as well, while my friends were more connected to what I really needed." While Leda's family was trapped in the same cycle of grief, moving through the motions of what it means to lose a relative so unexpectedly and traumatically, her friends were taking action. They were loving her.

But for all the love that Leda felt, she also experienced disappointment as close friends fell short with their care, revealing that they didn't really understand that now was the time to act.

A close friend of Leda's, who was living overseas at the time she lost Marlowe, called Leda in the early days and made her a promise: she would phone every day with a new task, an assignment to help her reach the end of each day. The first task Leda was assigned was writing in a journal, which she did.

"I remember feeling so thankful for her, words couldn't explain it," Leda tells me. "But then she just didn't do it. She didn't call me every day. She didn't set me tasks. She didn't understand how much I was banking on that, really needed it." Every day, Leda's resentment built up, little by little, until she found herself constantly ruminating on what this friend, along with two or three others, should have been doing and saying but weren't. Finally, it all got too much. Leda texted her friend and told her that she didn't want to hear from her again. Instead of waiting for the calls that never seemed to come, Leda decided to end things herself.

Still, Leda is understanding of the situation. Caring for a friend isn't easy, especially when it comes to grief and loss. "I often think back on how I acted when a friend lost one of their parents, or something else bad happened, and I just think, 'God, I really didn't get it.' And I feel bad about that." Now, she knows firsthand the difference a friend's care can make.

"I wouldn't be here without my friends. If I hadn't spoken to them about how I felt, I don't think I could have tried for another baby. My marriage might not have made it through, because your partner can't be your everything," Leda says. "I don't want to say I've healed, because you don't heal from this shit, but I'm able to cope because of their care."

Every conversation I've had with Leda since she lost Marlowe, alongside countless conversations with people I'm not personally close to but who have been held tightly in times of need, has only confirmed something I've long suspected to be true: Nobody can care for us in the same way as our friends.

In 2000, psychologist Shelley Taylor and her team of researchers from the University of California presented the "tend and befriend" theory,[8] which coexists with the well-known fight-or-flight response. The tend-and-befriend concept builds on observations that under conditions of threat, many humans tend to their offspring, to ensure their survival, but also connect with others, looking to find joint protection and comfort.

According to Taylor, stress research that focuses primarily on the fight-or-flight response ignores the fact that humans are social by nature, and according to that logic, it makes more sense that we would tend to one another's needs and band together rather than fight threats or flee on our own. This alternative to fight-or-flight, a response that elicits stress, simultaneously reduces stress-related health threats, especially when occurring over the long term.

During their research, Taylor's team mainly—though not exclusively—cited tending and befriending behavior in women, dating back to human evolution from hunter-gatherer groups. With that in mind, when you consider that almost all of the scientific research on stress before the 1990s excluded women completely, it becomes clear why it may have taken so long for this alternative response to stress to become recognized.

In a modern context, the tend-and-befriend theory explains the way I've seen people come together through difficult times. During the COVID-19 pandemic, people offered to shop for unwell, elderly, or immunocompromised neighbors. During natural disasters, like wildfires and floods, people offer strangers their labor and spare rooms. Whenever I've worked in a team facing a difficult restructuring or a round of layoffs, friendships have always emerged through that time of intense stress. To me, each of these scenarios proves that, for many of us, the decision to stay and fight or flee a difficult situation almost always comes after assessing how we can care for the people around us.

Five weeks after Leda lost Marlowe, she got a DM on Instagram from a woman named Jade, the sister-in-law of one of Leda's friends. A couple of months earlier, Jade had given birth to stillborn twins, Alfie and Mimi. Once Jade and Leda started talking, they never stopped. "We share everything with each other. I think once you go through a tragedy with someone by your side, you're kind of bonded for life," Leda tells me. What was at first a text friendship took on a new form when the two women found themselves in the same grief support group. When Leda entered the room and saw Jade for the first time, standing at the opposite side, she walked toward her with open arms.

When Leda and Jade both became pregnant again, Leda a few months after Jade, they both moved into a new support group called Pregnancy After Loss Support, or PALS for short. When Leda tells me and other old friends about the women she's grown close to in that group, she refers to them as her "pals," and we know who she's referencing without a second thought. The kind of grief work these parents do in PALS, with pals, is difficult. The purpose of this kind of counseling is to help get you ready for your next baby. In each session, expectant parents are asked to face their grief head on. "They force you to recognize that yes, you did lose a baby, but this one is going to be here soon, and it's going to need you," says Leda. While the parents in the group consider how they will tend to their next baby through their grief, they are also befriending each other.

In June 2022, Leda gave birth to her second son, River. Of the five friends Leda met in PALS, she's still close with two of them. They talk every day in a group chat Leda says would be deeply alarming to anyone who doesn't know what it's like to lose a baby. "All we do is talk about really inappropriate stuff," she tells me. "We make it funny—it can happen."

When I visit Leda, it's the week she's returned to work after taking parental leave. She tells me how after dropping River at a nearby day care, she returned home to log online for work, but immediately broke down before she could even get to her laptop. Walking into her home, filled with River's things, but without her baby in her arms, prompted old feelings to come flooding back. The first thing she did was message her pals. "After you lose a baby, everything is different. We talk about everything because everything is skewed now," she says. Returning to work as the parent of a baby is always going to be uniquely complex, but for Leda and other parents who have experienced stillbirth or infant loss, the pool of friends who can relate to their feelings—and care for them accordingly—is dramatically smaller.

"You've got to find your people," Leda tells me. "If you don't, you're never going to be fully understood."

Big care, small care

In *Care: The Radical Art of Taking Time*,[9] Brooke McAlary presents her own scale of care. At one end of her scale, she describes what she calls "Big Care," which is the kind of care that revolves solely around "complex, global problems that dominate the headlines," like climate change, racial injustice, and social inequality. At the other end of the spectrum, according to McAlary, sits self-care, a kind of care that has, in recent years, strayed a long way from its roots.

In her 1988 book of essays *A Burst of Light*,[10] Audre Lorde wrote, "Caring for myself is not self-indulgence, it is self-preservation, and that is an act of political warfare." In her experience as a Black queer woman, this self-care allowed her the energy to fight for change. But thanks to the commodified version of self-care—the three-hundred-dollar facials, the weekend retreats, the *luxury* involved with "taking care of yourself"—the meaning behind the term has changed. The kind of radical self-care Lorde wrote about, with Black feminist origins, is distinct from the kind of care many people today are referring to when they use the term. If each of us were to stop and think of the ways we care for ourselves, we'd likely be able to bring to mind conflicting instances of practicing different kinds of care. There's self-care as a preservation tactic, which might look like removing ourselves from situations where we don't feel safe or supported, skipping events which we know will leave us depleted. And there is self-care as a participation in capitalism, which I will openly admit I take part in often.

McAlary isn't looking to discredit the importance of self-care, or society's collective need to care about the injustices that both demand and deserve our attention. She believes that the urge to care about the world's biggest problems and to look after ourselves while doing so are two worthy pursuits, but neither should ever be our sole focus. To think only about the world's big issues through Big Care, can leave us overwhelmed and exhausted to the point of total inaction—a feeling familiar to anyone who has read an Intergovernmental Panel on Climate Change (IPCC) report and found themselves temporarily incapable of caring about anything else. On the flip side, to focus only on self-care would be to exclude the people who need us, encouraging us to rely on often misguided therapy-speak tactics to prove to ourselves and others that it's perfectly fine for us to put ourselves first.

In her book, McAlary works to highlight the importance of what exists on the spectrum between Big Care and self-care, which she refers to as Small Care. Unlike Big Care or self-care, Small Care is a focus on how we can help ourselves and others through tiny acts of kindness. McAlary describes the joy of picking up garbage on the beach, collecting fresh flowers from her garden for her mom, and smiling at a stranger on the street. Each tiny act, she writes, was not just a choice to care, but was life-affirming.

After reading McAlary's book, I started noticing that when it comes to conversations about care, society fixates on Big Care and self-care, whether those exact terms are being used or not. Not seeming to *care* about the planet on Instagram and in everyday conversation is somehow worse than not taking any direct action against climate change and the companies and political parties that are responsible for it. Caring only about the big stuff—shareable Instagram graphics and all— without considering how we can become activists in our own communities, provide mutual aid or care for those within our families and friendship groups, isn't going to result in a safer, healthier, or more equal world.

One of the great secret joys of Small Care is that it is easily reciprocated. In a relatively selfish sense, this is the kind of care that's most likely to come back to you. When I ask Leda about whether or not she'd thought about how she'd cared for her friends before she lost Marlowe, she says she has—a lot. "I've definitely thought, *Fuck I'm glad I was a good friend to people*, because now I'm getting it back tenfold." Reciprocity, whether it's a mutual exchange of time, gifts, or emotional labor, is one of the most important foundations of true friendship. And it's deeply aligned with care.

Though what Leda's friends have done for her in the last two years could qualify as the kind of Small Care McAlary writes about, they have had a large impact. And while I haven't been through anything comparable to Leda's loss, I can still think of countless times Leda has cared for me in this way. And it all adds up. When I lived near Leda in my early twenties, she would leave her spare key out for me at least once a week, so I could go to her place and do my laundry. My house didn't have room for a washing machine, and every trip to Leda's meant thirty dollars saved at the laundromat, at a time when that kind of money really made a difference. On weekends, whether she was home or not, I'd go to her place, set myself up on her couch and wait for the spin cycle to end, helping myself to snacks she might have left me in the fridge. For Leda, hundreds of acts of Small Care for tens of different friends left her with a huge group of people who were ready to show up when she needed them. When it comes to care, the saying "what goes around comes around" couldn't be more true. Caring for our friends, both new and old, is the best thing we can do if we hope that, one day, they can care for us in return. Care isn't easy and it doesn't happen automatically. If you want to be cared for in the future, the best thing you can do is start caring for your friends, even the newest or most casual, right now.

In recent years, I have made peace with the fact that I expect a lot from my friends. I know that not everyone cares about their birthday, but I will always want a text on mine. If I am having surgery, I'd like to think my friends will check the time on the day and think of me, hoping that I'm not feeling any pain. I want the lint picked off my sweater, an eyelash brushed from my cheek. I want my hand to be gently held and to feel like there will always be a shared understanding that when I say something "isn't a big deal" it probably is, to me. I want my friends to expect all those same things from me, because if care doesn't sit warm in the heart of our friendship, I'm not sure I want it at all.

6

In the Group Chat

A ll of my friends live inside my phone. When I am home alone, I carry them with me from room to room. Every morning, I wake hungry for them, reaching to my bedside table to find out if they have left any updates for me, sprinkled like breadcrumbs through the apps I check multiple times every hour. If my friends haven't had anything to share, either directly with me or on social media, I check what my friends of friends are doing, then people I haven't met, then people I most definitely will never meet, unless in a chance celebrity encounter at a restaurant.

Though I, like everyone, have days of feeling isolated from my friends, on others it's as if there's no limit to our connection, regardless of the time or where in the world a friend may be. In the morning, I send a text to a friend about a reality TV finale that's airing that night. Before lunch, I voice memo back and forth with a different friend, covering everything from an abortion she had a decade ago to the symptoms and signs of polycystic ovary syndrome. In the afternoon, another friend updates me on the two gifts he's bought his boyfriend for his thirtieth birthday—I am sent screenshot images of both. On Instagram, I heart-react a friend's update that she's finally getting a refund from a clothing brand that mislabeled her package. I'm emailed an invitation to a friend's daughter's second birthday, so I put a reminder in the online calendar I share with my partner. All before 3 PM.

"How do you think your interactions with your close friends online differ compared to interactions with them offline?" This was the key question researchers asked in a 2022 study titled "Connecting with close friends online: A qualitative analysis of young adults' perceptions of online and offline social interactions with friends."[1] Of the 627 people interviewed, 567 noted that there was a difference between their online and offline interactions with their friends. When researchers filtered through the participants' answers, they found a number of recurring themes. For example, something many of us love about interacting with friends online is the sense of control we have over the conversation. We can write back to a text later (or not at all), consider what we want to say before taking the time to type and rework it, and craft the image we want to present to new and potential friends online, whether it be on Instagram, TikTok, or Twitter/X. It all sounds very calculated, but in reality, it's something most of us—myself included—do habitually almost every day.

Despite the opportunity for forethought online communication provides, one of the most common distinctions people in the study made about their conversations with close friends online and off is that they were more likely to have deeper and richer discussions in person. According to the participants, online chats were often about checking in, making plans, and keeping in touch until they could see their friends in person. A twenty-two-year-old woman who was part of the study explained, "I find it easier to make conversation online, but the connection doesn't feel real." It's an answer I relate to, calling to mind the longing I feel for a friend when it's been too long between in-person catch-ups, no matter how many hours we've spent texting, sending voice memos, or speaking on the phone in between.

But this isn't the case for everyone. For some people, the accessibility that the internet affords our friendships can override all else. For others, the lack of nonverbal cues, which was quoted in the study as being detrimental to online interactions, can actually make conversations with friends easier and much less stressful. Like everything to do with friendship, it's complex.

Viewing online relationships as supplementary is a privilege. For people living with disabilities, long-term illness, or chronic pain, the internet creates a vital bridge between them and their friends. It can play a similar role in a lot of other friendships, whether people find themselves separated from their friends by distance or are looking to find new friendships with people they're unlikely to meet in person. On the internet, intimate friendships can grow into vast and sweeping online communities. Social identity theory, first proposed by psychologist Henri Tajfel in the 1970s,[2] is based on the idea that being part of a group contributes to a person's sense of self and belonging. Online, it's no different. Whether they've lived with a health condition or had a niche interest, as long as people have had access to the internet, they've used it to create spaces where group members can feel a collective sense of unity and togetherness.

New place, new online space

In September 2018, nine friends who had met at a Chinese-language school in Melbourne decided to start a Facebook group. All in their late teens and early twenties, the friends first bonded in class, often joking about their shared experiences as Asian-Australians. But it wasn't until they came across another Facebook group, "Subtle Private School Traits," that they decided to start their own. Their group, "Subtle Asian Traits," now has more than 1.9 million members, making it one of the biggest online Asian communities in the world.

The idea behind the group—much like other "Subtle Traits" groups that have come before and after it—is to share jokes that other people with Asian heritage can relate to. Primarily, this is done through memes posted to the Facebook group, its public offshoot, and the brand's Instagram page. On the Subtle Asian Traits website you can now buy branded T-shirts, hoodies, and tote bags. All of this exists to celebrate the "similarities and differences within Asian culture and subcultures." And it does exactly that.

In an interview with *The New York Times*[3] a few months after the group's launch, cofounder Anne Gu spoke of the tediousness of answering questions about her heritage, explaining that the group provides a safe haven in which members can share their experiences. "We don't have to explain stuff," she said. But the group isn't just about relatability, it's about real connection. Founded by friends, Subtle Asian Traits has also brought new friends together.

Whitney Chan, a social media specialist in her thirties, is used to meeting people through Facebook. When she moved from Sydney to the UK, she quickly discovered and joined two groups: the London Lonely Girls Club and London New Girl. Before Whitney moved she already had a friend living in London, though her apartment was at the opposite end of the city. Whitney's sister lived in the city too, but she still felt determined to carve out her own friendship circle, as helpful as her sister was when it came to getting settled. Beyond the company and guidance her sister could provide, she was looking for friends who shared her unique interests and were potentially also new to London.

Inside the Facebook groups, things can feel a little like

online dating. You put your best self forward, see who feels compatible, then try to forge a connection. Often the next step after connecting on Facebook is forming a WhatsApp group of people (in this case women) who live in a similar area—which is exactly what Whitney did. "I was really nervous. I'd never done anything like that—putting myself out there. I thought, 'no one's going to join,' but I put the WhatsApp link in the group and people started joining," she tells me. Once the group was formed, they started making plans. If there was a new rooftop bar someone wanted to go to, they'd see who else in the group was free. There were drag brunches and a lot of picnics. Once, the group went to a comedy show, and when the comedian asked another group of girls in the crowd how they all knew each other, their answer was the same as Whitney's group: through Facebook.

London, much like New York, is a city of going out rather than staying in. So when Whitney left the UK to move to the US, she felt the same pull to make new friends. During her second week living in New York, one of Whitney's friends tagged her in a post that had been shared in Subtle Asian Traits, along with another group she was also a member of, Subtle Asian Cooking. The post was an invitation to a potluck dinner hosted by a group member in Brooklyn. Whitney was exhausted from the move and from the summer heat, but neither felt like a good enough reason not to go. So she cooked a pot of coconut noodles and went to the party.

When Whitney arrived at the apartment, there were nine or ten other people there. By the time she left, after hours of picking over everything from store-bought donuts to homemade char siu, more than forty people had squeezed inside, then overflowed onto the building's rooftop. Unlike other Asian meetups she'd been to before, cultural identity wasn't at the center of the conversations. Instead, questions about where they or their family were from were passing comments, made on the way toward deeper and more satisfying discussions. Whitney had plans to meet her boyfriend at a nearby dive bar after the potluck later that night, so she asked the group she'd been chatting with if they'd like to join her. They did. And the party continued into the night. When I ask Whitney if she's still in touch with anyone from that event, her face lights up on my laptop screen. "Funnily enough, I hung out with a friend last night who was one of the girls I met at the potluck," she says. "So yeah, we definitely still hang out."

Groups, along with events and birthday reminders, are now considered one of Facebook's last redeeming qualities. While most of us have only a bunch of embarrassing tagged photos and status updates to show for our time on the social media site, Whitney has something much richer. She has friends from London, her New York potluck friends, and friends from other online groups. If you're looking for meaningful social connections, Facebook still has something to offer.

The internet meetup isn't a new concept, though. For decades, fans of certain bands, celebrities, and film franchises have used their internet connection as a means of finding people who share their obsession, before making plans to gather together in the real world. Today, I see people who use the same fitness apps, listen to the same podcasts, or read the same Substack newsletters turn their online connection into real-life friendships by getting together in person. In most online spaces lies the opportunity to create real, meaningful connections offline. When making friends, a shared interest or identity can go a long way, and the easiest way to press fast-forward on these friendships can be to arrange a meetup.

Making friend requests

What does it mean to be friends with someone? Thanks to social media, the online world offers a complex landscape of social connection. There are Facebook friends, TikTok mutuals, and Instagram followers. Sometimes, the distinction between being a part of somebody's audience and being their friend isn't as clear as it ought to be; the line between being a follower and a friend can be easily blurred.

In *Trick Mirror: Reflections on Self-Delusion*,[4] Jia Tolentino writes about the way social media encourages us to seek rewards from the people we're connected with online. "This is why everyone tries to look so hot and well-traveled on Instagram; this is why everyone seems so smug and triumphant on Facebook; this is why, on Twitter, making a righteous political statement has come to seem, for many people, like a political good in itself," she writes.

When I think about the difficulties of making and keeping friends, I don't often consider how easy it can be to request, follow or like someone on social media. With the vulnerability and effort that friend making usually requires stripped away, the ease with which we can make "friends" online can begin to feel a little hollow. Every time I log on to an app, I'm presented with suggestions for new people I should follow or befriend. These people are usually a friend of a friend, or someone the algorithm assumes I'll be interested in.

Whether intentional or not, social media and these kinds of connections in each of our digital networks homogenize friendships in a specific way that wouldn't have occurred in the past. And while some exclusively online friendships can bloom and continue to grow, there's no denying that social media has made it much easier to turn friendship into performance.

In *Hanging Out: The Radical Power of Killing Time*,[5] Sheila Liming writes about what she calls "Facebook parties." Attending a small college in Ohio in 2005, Liming was first introduced to the site when accounts were only available to American college students, linked to the schools they were attending. Before Facebook's arrival, whenever a party was being planned, handwritten or printed invitations would be left in students' decorative brass letterboxes, which were located in the center of the campus. The letterboxes were so small they were checked several times a day; unlike an Instagram DMs folder, they were only big enough to hold a couple of invitations, notes, or love letters at a time.

As Facebook fever spread through the campus, these del-
icately crafted invitations, often printed in the university
library, were delivered less and less often. Facebook parties became commonplace so quickly and so seamlessly that
Liming began to call any party organized the traditional way,
by printed invitation or word-of-mouth, a "non-Facebook
party."

But it wasn't just the manner in which people were invited
that defined a Facebook party, it was also how people acted
at them. "People started to collect friends, experiences, and
parties like trading cards, hoarding them away in their online
personality silos," Liming writes in *Hanging Out*. "The parties themselves, they stopped being about having fun and
started being primarily about *looking* like you were having
fun—about advertising your own capacity to have fun." An
important aspect of any Facebook party, according to Liming,
was the photos taken throughout the night with the purpose
of being posted online the following day. I didn't start college
until 2009, but even years later and on the other side of the
world, the phenomenon Liming describes is eerily relatable.
To go to a party in the early years of Facebook was to attend
with the desperate hope of being tagged in a handful of photos in the days or weeks that followed. If you were lucky, one
would be good enough to become your new profile photo. It
wasn't uncommon for my friends and me to spend the entire
night with digital cameras strapped to our wrists, planning
to log on to Facebook the next morning, bleary-eyed, upload
our selections, and tag away.

These days, invitations don't come through my own Facebook account as often as they once did, as friends move away from the platform, and other digital options like Paperless Post take its place. Still, the effects of the "Facebook party" feel impossible to shake. While I haven't had a friend upload a photo album to Facebook in years, we still dress for each event knowing we may be photographed, posted, tagged, reacted to, and commented on. We party in person knowing it may very well lead to being perceived online. As Liming writes, "Today, of course, every party is a Facebook party, even if it has nothing whatsoever to do with Facebook." The way social media has changed the way we spend time together in person can't be ignored. I've chosen restaurants because they have good lighting, so I can place a friend's cocktail close to a plate of oysters—before we taste either—to take a photo. I'm not too ashamed to admit that everything from my picnic blanket to salad bowl to couch cushions have all been purchased with the knowledge that they will one day be photographed and posted on social media in the midst of hanging out with friends.

But if I really dig into the insecurities that fuel my decisions to spend my money and style my life in-case-of-photo, what's perhaps most confronting is the knowledge that I'm far from alone in feeling this way. The idea behind the Facebook party has changed everything about the way we plan to spend time with our friends—at home, at parties, in restaurants—whether we like it or not. And social media has changed the way we want people to see us. It can also be deceptive. In *Thinking, Fast and Slow*,[6] Daniel Kahneman describes a cognitive bias he calls "What You See Is All There Is." Essentially, this phenomenon explains the way we jump to conclusions and easy explanations—deducing that the information we have available is the only information there is. On social media, this can play out in a number of different ways. An Instagram post thanking a friend for always being there doesn't hold space for insecurities or disagreements of the past. Friends who appear to constantly catch up for themed dinner parties and wholesome weekends away don't post about the arguments that happened while planning each holiday or the friend who felt left out as soon as they arrived at dinner. Screenshots of group chats can make it look as though friends are in constant contact with a Rolodex of personal jokes when in reality, the chat could have been lying dormant for weeks before that day. Even within our friendships, we use social media to portray the reality we hope to wish into existence—and the people who follow us can't help but believe the white lies we all sometimes tell.

With the exception of fleeting TikTok trends that encourage users to show their "true selves," it's rare to see friends sitting at home on a Saturday night flicking through their five different streaming services before deciding there's nothing to watch and going to bed. We don't see other people while they're scrolling on their phone, wondering why they didn't get invited to that long lunch. Social media, by definition, encourages social connection but it simultaneously facilitates exclusion.

Finding an internet connection

A former coworker once told me she had added all her closest friends to Apple's Find My Friends. Any day at any time, she could open the app and see exactly where her friends were, guess where they might be going, and sometimes see who they were with. At first, I was skeptical. The concept of tracking friends felt like an invasion of privacy, an easy way to create a world in which nobody could ever really be alone. But eventually, I came around. My coworker's logic was that, in a city like New York, it can feel impossible to replicate the closeness of a small town or suburb. By sharing their locations, her group of friends were more likely to have "chance" encounters after realizing they were both close to the same lunch spot or both at home on a Sunday afternoon.

When I was still living in my hometown, it wasn't hard to figure out where my friends were. I'd walk past their work and either see them behind the register or waiting tables—or I wouldn't. When I drove home, I might see their car parked outside their house, or the house of whoever they were dating at the time. Without much conscious effort, I'd see almost everyone I knew most Saturday nights when we went to the one nightclub in town. Staying in touch was easy because running into each other regularly was a given, as we had fewer places to be. But as times have changed, so have our friendships.

When Kristen S. He realized she was transgender, she was living alone in Melbourne. While quarantining through the

COVID pandemic, she developed a strong sense that something was missing in her life. "Despite being in touch with really great friends and trying to keep busy, I just felt a void," she tells me over the phone, thirteen months after starting hormone replacement therapy (HRT). "I spent a lot of 2021 searching for what that void was."

One evening, eating dinner alone, Kristen realized she'd been a trans girl her entire life. And while it felt like everything was crashing down around her, it also felt like everything was falling into place. She finally felt she had an explanation for her personality quirks, her attitude, her relationships—all the things that people around her may have never noticed but which were now so obvious to her. Since that moment, things have been good. "It takes a lot less energy to be myself than to put up walls and pretend to be something I'm not," she says. Coming out was, in Kristen's own words, an unburdening.

As we chat, Kristen mentions her friend Hannah, a fellow trans music journalist who lives in New York, but it's not until midway through our conversation that she realizes Hannah was the first person she came out to, despite their not being particularly close at the time. They'd been in touch for over a year on Twitter/X, bonding over music and artists they both loved, but had never really gotten deep. Still, the moment she realized she was trans, she decided to message Hannah.

When I speak to Hannah, it's getting late in New York and she's on Zoom from her apartment in the Upper East Side. "Kristen and I had DM'd a couple of times because we have a lot in common, but then one day she writes to me and says, 'Oh, guess whose egg just cracked?'" Hannah tells me. "I'm still not entirely sure how we became as close as we have, which is very amusing to me."

Hannah and Kristen are both attracted to women and tell me that a lot of their friendship revolves around sending photos of celebrity crushes back and forth, then responding either with gender envy or their go-to hypnotized eyes emoji. These expressions of desire are wholesome, according to Kristen—a practice that was denied to them both in their past lives. Now that they've both reconciled themselves hormonally and socially, they're happy to be making up for lost time on Twitter/X. "People say no art exists in a vacuum. In a similar way, friendships are what makes all these moments of joy feel so much more real and reflective," says Kristen.

In our separate conversations, Kristen and Hannah both mention a feature Kristen wrote for *Junkee*[7] profiling the indie pop band MUNA. In her interview with the band, Kristen writes about the way queer people often find themselves mirrored in one another. It's not lost on me that both Hannah and Kristen—queer friends and music journalists—feel the same way about one another. "Kristen and I are very similar, but we're not the same person. We don't want to be each other and we don't need anything from each other," says Hannah. "A misconception is that trans friends don't have anything in common other than being trans, but Kristen and I have a lot of other things in common. We're really fascinated by each other."

Kristen and Hannah's friendship is one of many trans friendships both women now have. For them, online friendships have been a source of fun, connection, and in some cases, life-changing information.

Years ago, Hannah tweeted a map of informed-consent clinics in America for people starting HRT. She promptly forgot about the tweet until she started DMing with a new friend, Darcy, only to find out that the reason Darcy was able to start hormones was because of the map that Hannah tweeted. In safe pockets of sites like Twitter/X and Reddit, on private accounts and in well-moderated forums, you never know which of your online friends you could be helping.

Social media can amplify feelings of loneliness but can also make us feel less lonely. It can connect us in times we would otherwise have been completely separated. It makes meeting people and making plans easier, because it has changed the very definition of what it means to be somebody's "friend" and to spend time with them. An awareness of the difficulties technology is capable of creating, along with a knowledge of the joy that's to be found within it, are the only things that can really guide us on our way to using the internet to build brighter friendships—whether they ever exist in 3D or not.

Hanging out in a virtual reality

The internet lifts our inhibitions in ways that can make connection feel seamless and smooth as silk, but it simultaneously allows people to act with vitriol and cruelty. The downside of finding connection in an unexpected place can be opening a Pandora's box of things to hate about yourself and everyone else. Technology can make people feel close, then distant. It can make us feel loved, then hated. Such is the dichotomy of social media, of the internet, and, at times, of friendship.

Between long working hours, family commitments, and household chores, our energy for in-person activities can dwindle. If you're someone who once relied on your netball club for your weekly socializing but then stopped playing, online spaces that replicate that club environment can be a very welcome solution.

We Met in Virtual Reality,[8] an HBO documentary released in 2022, was filmed entirely in virtual reality. The film introduces people who are hanging out in the online platform VRChat as avatars of their own choosing. Though the documentary was filmed in 2020, some of the people interviewed have been hanging out in VRChat since 2018, participating in such varied activities as teaching sign language classes, belly dancing, enjoying Friday night drinks, and falling in love. As one avatar named Jenny explains in the film, "Making friends here is sometimes what saves people's lives or what gets them up out of bed in the morning."

Friends who exist primarily online, whether on social media or in a virtual reality, are often judged by people who don't have firsthand experience of this type of connection. But friendships that exist only or primarily online can be just as valid, attentive, caring, and life-affirming as those that exist offline.

In her novel *Tomorrow, and Tomorrow, and Tomorrow*,[9] Gabrielle Zevin writes of the vulnerability of gaming with someone online, which I believe can be applied to many online friendships. "To allow yourself to play with another person is no small risk," she writes. "It means allowing yourself to be open, to be exposed, to be hurt. It is the human equivalent of the dog rolling on its back—*I know you won't hurt me, even though you can*. It is the dog putting its mouth around your hand and never biting down. To play requires trust and love." As our friendships take new shapes, the trust that a friend will take care with your online self just as tenderly as they would the real you is vital. As friendships evolve, it's imperative that kindness and connection remain key pillars of our most important relationships, whether they seek to complement in-person interactions or replace them entirely.

7

Working It Out

The canteen was quieter than usual the day before I lost my job. People were whispering in person and quietly typing on Slack about mergers and restructures and rumors they'd apparently heard from someone in the elevator. Something just felt off. That evening, I insisted that my partner and I have beans on toast for dinner.

I'd found the recipe—if you can call it that—on the very website from which I was about to be laid off. "Rice and beans is a joke of cheap eating, but it's also the gospel," Jaime Green wrote. "And the way I learned to love the humble legume, in my own carefully budgeted cooking, was through bodega beans."[1] The concept behind "bodega beans," originally written about in a 2007 post on the food blog *The Amateur Gourmet*,[2] was that you could buy every ingredient for this cheap and allegedly delicious meal at your local bodega (corner shop). Following the vague recipe felt like all I could do to keep my mind off the storm I could feel rolling in. I sautéed a little garlic and some onion in a pan with olive oil, added a can of white beans, then seasoned everything with salt and pepper. Once they were warmed, I served my beans on two slices of buttered toast.

Before I'd even taken a bite, I saw the email notification flash on my phone screen: a round of major layoffs was coming, and my team would likely be affected. I looked down at the beans, hoping to feel grateful for the fact that I hadn't received this news minutes after ordering expensive takeout or while sitting in a restaurant waiting to be served a twenty-eight-dollar pasta I could easily have made at home. Instead, I felt depressed. To top it all off, the beans tasted like shit.

That first time I was laid off I didn't just lose my job, I also lost my visa. During the three months it took me to find a new job—and an accompanying permission slip to stay in the country—I spent every day applying for every role that I was remotely qualified for, along with a few I definitely wasn't. I spent afternoons watching teen dramas on Netflix and miserably texting my group chat I had with my former team, who were also living out the same lather-rinse-repeat cycle of unemployment. Each day without a tether to the country I was living in was hard, but not seeing my work friends every day was excruciating. When I'd first arrived in the US, I'd taken for granted how lucky I was to have clicked with my coworkers so instantly—they weren't just new friends in a new country, they were new friends with whom I was able to spend forty hours a week typing, laughing, and gossiping.

The media company we'd all worked for promoted friendship in the office; so much so that we were encouraged to think of our colleagues as family. The canteen was expansive, with large tables made for groups of rowdy twentysomethings; holiday parties went late into the night; and team outings and happy hours weren't only tolerated but encouraged (and often expensed on corporate credit cards). When the company dissolved our team—cutting us off from the family it had forced us to create—it felt like they were trying to dissolve our friendships too.

We also happened to be in the middle of a demonic New York winter. On one of my worst days, I walked four blocks in 8°F weather to buy myself a houseplant as a reward for hitting a new milestone of job applications. Within hours of getting home, the plant's leaves had turned black, its frozen cells defrosting and killing it from the inside out. That wilted peace lily sat on my coffee table for days, a reminder of the fragility of hope. Thankfully, weeks before my visa timed out, I found another job. I worked there, and loved it, until deciding to leave the US of my own accord in late 2020 for obvious global pandemic–related reasons. I was excited to be back in Australia, where my stability wouldn't be so wholly tied to my employment, though I soon learned that there was a lot more I should have wished for.

My new job was as the editor in chief at a different media company. But after almost two years, I was laid off again. After I got the news, my partner and I went out for dinner. I ordered us rounds of margaritas and didn't once consider whether we had tins of beans or a lone brown onion waiting for us at home. I wasn't worried about my visa or money or security; I felt free. To lose a job that felt like just that—a job—rather than one that felt like a family was easier to stomach.

Two days later, on the afternoon of my final day of employment, I logged off early and went to the pub. Three former members of my team—all women in their late twenties and early thirties, all still employed by the company I was hours away from officially leaving—came to join me. Over three bottles of wine, I thought of what I'd learned about these women while working alongside them, and how different our conversations were from the wistful ones I'd shared with coworkers three years earlier.

These were friendships I was sure I could carry into the next chapter of my life, but before I'd even been locked out of my email account, I knew there would be no longing for the days when we'd all sat side by side. Rather than the joyous icing on top of a job I loved, as has been the case at previous workplaces, these friendships had functioned as a protective blanket that helped us all get through each arduous day of confusion and pivoting directions. Instead of being encouraged to consider our company a family, as I had felt in my previous role, we'd created a workplace family on our own terms.

That afternoon, we spoke a little about the company I was leaving, what it would look like without me, and of the work we'd all done together. But mostly we spoke of care. Who would need the most comfort in my absence? How would the remaining staff link together to build a safety net to protect themselves for what could possibly come next?

Walking home from the pub that night, I thought of everything I knew about the people on my team: breakups, unwell parents, and endometriosis diagnoses that meant necessary days in bed and hard-to-get appointments. After two years, I left my job with pockets full of emotional breadcrumbs that I'd collected, one by one, after countless meetings, Zoom calls, and "I won't be in today, I'm so sorry" texts. In 2019, I'd packed up my desk wondering: *What's next for me?* But this time, I left thinking only: *What about them?* In the workplace I'd just farewell'd, friendship wasn't a social perk, a way to occupy long days and make lunch breaks fun—it was a means of survival.

Leaning on each other

Back in 2013, two years after I got my first job working in magazines, Sheryl Sandberg's *Lean In: Women, Work, and the Will to Lead*[3] promised to help women thrive at work. But not by implementing any changes in the workplace itself. According to the former Facebook COO, it was women who had to start doing things differently if they ever wanted to get ahead. Sandberg's approach to work, brimming with what would eventually be known as "girlboss" behavior, overlooked the broader systemic issues that exist in the workplace. It generally ignored the experiences of women of color, nonbinary people, and trans women, along with economic inequality and the kind of deeply entrenched sexism that can't be solved by adopting a "power pose."

For a long time, my own identity and self-worth were so closely bound with my career success that from a distance, all three might as well have been measuring the same thing. It makes sense that, through these years, I didn't feel like anyone could understand me as well as my work friends. They knew what it meant to get "senior" added to my job title, even if that so-called promotion didn't come with a pay raise. They got why I so firmly believed the work I was doing wasn't just meaningful but necessary.

My work friends understood it all, because they felt the same way. I didn't need to justify long hours or bad pay to them or explain why I stayed at a publishing company that was so clearly crumbling, because they were there with me on deadline nights, their bank accounts were equally empty, and they were hanging on just as tightly to the promise we'd all been sold about how lucky we were to have the jobs we did. My work has always meant a lot to me, and so have the friends I've worked with. But while my relationship to the workplace has since changed, the importance I place on work friends is as strong as ever.

In recent years, there's been a culture-wide shift in how many people view work. I know I'm not alone in feeling less motivated by promotions and meaningless perks and more inspired by companies that offer flexible working arrangements and competitive leave policies. The so-called "great resignation"—a term coined by Anthony Klotz,[4] a professor of management at University College London's School of Management—saw record numbers of people in the US quit their jobs in 2021 and 2022. According to the *Harvard Business Review*,[5] five key factors drove up these resignation statistics: retirement, which saw older workers leave the workforce at a younger age than they might have before the pandemic; relocation, as people left their role because they wanted to move elsewhere; reconsideration, in which people felt their approach to work change due to burnout or increased caretaking responsibilities; reshuffling, which accounted for people who quit their current role to find a new one; and reluctance, which saw people quit out of fear of contracting COVID or returning to a workplace that didn't offer remote or hybrid options.

Despite these resignations happening for a wide-ranging number of reasons, the figures spurred countless TikToks, essays, and somewhat oblivious LinkedIn posts from executives and recruitment specialists that suggested a more pointed motivation. When Kim Kardashian infamously said, "It seems like nobody wants to work these days," many people replied with a confused, "Well, why would we?"

According to the American Psychological Association's "2023 Work in America Survey," 77 percent of workers reported having experienced work-related stress in the past

month, with 57 percent of those experiencing feelings associated with burnout, like emotional exhaustion, a desire to quit,
a lack of motivation, and anger toward coworkers and cus-
tomers. Only two-fifths of workers surveyed believed their
employers offered a culture in which time off is respected.
Factor in a lack of health insurance with mental health cov-
erage, limited access to employee assistance programs, and
workplaces that are becoming less flexible than they were in
the past, and it's no wonder many people consider putting in
their resignation.

There are plenty of reasons for employees to feel dis-
heartened about the current state of work. Salaries aren't
increasing at the same rate as inflation, workforces are being
downsized as tasks are automated by machines or AI, and
a lack of government support and funding is leaving many
industries—from the arts to education—feeling as though
they're an inch from total collapse. But for a lot of other
people, it's as simple as this: people who feel lonely at work
are more likely to want to leave their jobs. And a whole lot of
people are feeling alone in the workplace right now.

In her book *The Lonely Century: A Call to Reconnect*,[6] econ-
omist Noreena Hertz offers an explanation as to why every
industry—not just those that have shifted to remote work—
are experiencing record levels of loneliness. "Part of the reason many of us feel so detached from our colleagues today
is because the quality of our communication with them is so
much shallower than in the past," she writes. As teams down-
size and workloads increase, our focus at work is more likely

to be on productivity than cultivating friendships. When you're overworked, as people across most industries are, it's hard to justify a coffee break or lengthy conversation with a colleague, client, or regular customer. As long as friendships aren't a measure of success in the workplace, they're never going to be a priority.

Technology's influence on workplace loneliness feels obvious: a Slack DM isn't as personable as visiting someone at their desk to ask them a question, and an email replacing a meeting, while preferable for people's productivity and time management, isn't going to involve the pre- and post-meeting chatter that helps make work interactions feel less transactional.

In her research, Hertz also found that modern workplace updates, like open-plan office layouts, had a negative effect on employee friendships. If you've ever worked in an open-plan office, especially those where hot desking (shared workspace) is either mandatory or encouraged, you'll likely be familiar with their eerie quiet. Though it sounds counterintuitive, research has found that workplaces with cubicles offer people the privacy they need to speak out loud to one another and, in turn, become closer.[7] Sitting next to a different person every day and worrying that every word you say can be heard by an entire office encourages people to keep quiet and keep to themselves. And the more we keep to ourselves, the more likely we are to take breaks alone, skip office happy hours, and avoid team lunches, which eventually end up feeling like a gathering of relative strangers.

As Hertz writes, "The loneliness of work is not only about feeling disconnected from the people we work with, whether our colleagues or our boss. It's also about feeling bereft of agency, feeling powerless." So many things are out of our control in the workplace, from our workload to our seating arrangements. The desire to belong is an inherently human experience and, if connection doesn't look possible from where we're currently standing, our instincts will push us to move somewhere else. When I speak to Dr. Michelle Lim, a clinical psychologist and loneliness researcher, about workplace friendships, she assures me that loneliness can be a necessary instigator for change. "Sometimes, loneliness is a prompt to do something different."

The opposite of loneliness is connection, just as the opposite of burnout is motivation, and the opposite of failure is success. After my call with Dr. Lim, I wonder: If the deep ache of loneliness can inspire us to look to friendship as a solution, why wouldn't that be just as possible with feelings of failure and workplace exhaustion? If leaning in isn't the answer, perhaps leaning on each other is.

Work can't love you back, but people can

In *Can't Even: How Millennials Became the Burnout Generation*,[8] Anne Helen Petersen digs deeper into ideas she first wrote about in her viral 2019 BuzzFeed essay on burnout, which put words to the way an entire generation were coming to understand their relationship with the workplace.[9] "We were raised to believe that if we worked hard enough, we could win the system—of capitalism and mediocrity—or at least live comfortably within it. But something happened in the late 2010s. We looked up from our work and realized, there's no winning the system when the system itself is broken," writes Petersen.

Much of Petersen's writing about burnout and the modern workplace rings true to me—sometimes painfully so—as it does to most millennials I know. In her book, Petersen writes that our shared desire for the "cool job" was a means of elevating a certain kind of labor to the point that we felt honored to be doing it. Many of us have been made to feel "lucky" to have a job that's deemed impressive, regardless of whether it's well paid or possible to be done within reasonable working hours. The desirability of these kinds of jobs, Petersen writes, is what makes them so unsustainable. When I was an editorial assistant earning thirty thousand dollars a year, nobody had to tell me that there were quite literally hundreds of young women who would have been happy to take my place, because I already knew. Not only that, I knew many of those women would have been more financially able to survive on that kind of salary—women whose family lived in the city or who had parents who could subsidize their rent—but I was determined to make it work. So I did—on a diet of ninety-cent garlic bread and the free food I could scavenge from around the office.

While acknowledging problems with the modern workplace is one thing, solving these issues is another. Joining workers' unions, advocating for better pay and improved rights, and setting boundaries around work hours and expectations can work to help find a solution, but there are no guarantees. And these pathways toward solutions often involve banding together with like-minded coworkers, further impressing the need for genuine workplace camaraderie.

In *Work Won't Love You Back: How Devotion to Our Jobs Keeps Us Exploited, Exhausted, and Alone*,[10] Sarah Jaffe writes that we have all been told that work itself is meant to bring us fulfillment, pleasure, meaning, and joy. "We're supposed to work for the love of it, and how dare we ask questions about the way our work is making other people rich while we struggle to pay rent and barely see our friends," she writes.

Much like the hierarchical nuclear family, workplace "families" can easily become dysfunctional and, in the worst instances, harmful. Jaffe believes that the modern expectation that we should all be "happy" at work demands emotional work from employees. "Work, after all, has no feelings," she writes. "Capitalism cannot love. This new work ethic, in which work is expected to give us something like self-actualization, cannot help but fail."

The cost of becoming a parent

It's not easy to be a mother in America. According to *Forbes*,[11] the average cost of childbirth in the US is 18,865 dollars, with that cost rising to 26,280 dollars if a C-section is required.

Before birthing parents return home from the hospital, they are overwhelmed, not just physically and emotionally, but financially too. And when it comes time to return to work (which American parents on average do sooner than parents living in similarly wealthy countries) things only get more difficult.

If you're not yet a parent, these kinds of statistics and figures can be overwhelming, to say the least. In 2019, researchers from the University of Sydney asked young people to imagine what will be important to the future success of their work and families. In an interview with the *Sydney Morning Herald*,[12] Elizabeth Hill, an associate professor in political economy at the University of Sydney, said that some women she spoke to in her research were actively deciding not to have kids after witnessing how many mothers struggle when returning to work.[13] "There seems to be an emerging group of young women who look around at their female colleagues and their workplaces and decide it is too hard to have children and a successful work life," Hill told the newspaper. In the US, things are no different, with a reported 33 percent[14] of women believing it's not viable to have a child while pursuing a career.

But what of those people who long to be parents and aren't willing to sacrifice that dream to the modern workplace? For me, it's one thing to acknowledge that parents, particularly those who have gone through pregnancy and childbirth, often return to a workplace that's not designed to support them, but it's another thing entirely to decide that the situation is so dire and unfixable that I'd give up having a child altogether. The corporate workplace wasn't designed with parents in mind. But while we wait for our workplaces or the government to offer solutions, like flexible working hours, affordable child care, or federal paid parental leave, people must do what they can to find their own—whether that's fair or not.

Cassandra Vozzo and Nikki Ronald, who have been friends for seven years, found an unexpected solution to balancing work and child care. After meeting while working on the same commercial sales team, they stayed in touch, even when Cass moved from the city back to her hometown after having her daughter, Ruby. One day, while talking on the phone, Cass mentioned a role she'd seen advertised and was thinking of applying for. As it turned out, Nikki, a mother of two, had already been in talks with a hiring manager about the same position. So, they hatched a plan.

"Nikki didn't want to do five days a week and I was only open to working three or four, so we thought, why don't we pitch a job share?" Cass tells me over the phone on her day off, after putting Ruby down for her midday nap. Together they worked on a presentation using examples of how job shares have worked for other people they knew in the industry, outlined their shared skill set, and highlighted the unique experience they'd each be able to bring to the table. In the past they'd worked in similar roles but had both since expanded their skills. They felt that the remote job share would be a way for the company to get all their experience combined, for the same price as one full-time salaried staffer. To them, it made sense for the company as well as their families, leaving them both with days off to care for their kids. The company agreed. They were hired.

When Cass and I speak, it's been a year since her job share with Nikki began. As other working parents have told me, one issue that arises with part-time work is the difficulty that can come with being able to maintain boundaries on your days off. As part of their arrangement, Nikki works Monday and Tuesday solo, overlapping with Cass on Wednesday, before Cass works Thursday and Friday on her own. For Cass, hearing from Nikki on one of her days off isn't as burdensome as it would be to hear from another colleague. "Because we're friends, it's fine for her to call me if she has a question. It can save her two hours of trying to figure something out," Cass says. "I know some people might not work like that, but we do."

Helping a friend at work will always feel more satisfying than helping a coworker you don't have a relationship with, but for Nikki and Cass, that feeling is even more amplified. They need each other to succeed, so they can remain a package deal. For Cass, her friendship with Nikki is what helped her return to the workforce in a way that felt manageable and even exciting. Their friendship became a solution to a problem that nobody—not corporations nor the government—appeared to be rushing to fix.

From work friends to business partners

There's something magic about the closeness that can be found in a workplace friendship. For people working with others in person, rather than remotely, these connections can become the closest adult equivalent of friendships made at school, in university dorms or in shared apartments. When you spend most of your day sitting or standing beside someone, it's easy to become accustomed to their habits, their likes and dislikes, and the tiny things that happen in their days, which they might not bother to mention to a friend outside work. When I've been close to friends at work, I've been privy to what they've dreamed about the night before, when they change their coffee order, when they have their period, when their hot water needs fixing, and what Airbnb they're booking for their upcoming weekend away. There's an intimacy that can only be found when occupying a physical space for so many hours a day. Shared with the right person, it can be precious.

Fourteen years into my career, many of my closest friends started as coworkers. The friends I've met at work, whether at the start of my career when I was still a teenager or now as I enter my thirties, make up a large portion of the friends who know me best. They were the people I was closest to— both physically and emotionally—when I first ran into my now long-term partner by chance at a party, when I became an aunt, when I started wearing glasses (a surprisingly big deal to me at the time), when I gave up meat for a year, and when a million other tiny but not insignificant events unfolded while I was at work. And while my work friends were there for so many moments that changed the course of my life, I was also there for theirs. Lunchtime walks, coffee runs, and tears in the bathroom on particularly bad days aside, there is a practicality that comes with work friendships. At work, making a new friend can mean finding someone to guide you, champion you and promote you. But the opposite can also apply. For people who start out as friends and then find themselves working together, there can be a completely different host of benefits.

When Erica Cerulo and Claire Mazur met in 2002, they were both undergrads at the University of Chicago. Claire was a freshman and Erica a sophomore, but they were quickly introduced by someone they now both jokingly refer to as a mutual frenemy. "We were very much alike," Claire tells me. "We had a lot in common and hit it off right away. I think we saw ourselves in each other."

Through college, the friends never technically worked together but were involved in some of the same extracurriculars that helped re-create a microcosm similar to many workplaces. As they worked together to bring music acts to campus—a role they both took incredibly seriously—they each got to witness what the other would be like in their future workplaces. There were budgets to manage, big egos to navigate, and teams to lead. Beyond their many shared interests outside college, the two quickly understood they had similar working styles when trying to get stuff done.

Moving to New York after college, the friends had the same experience as many twentysomethings who move to the city, figuring out who they were now and who they wanted to become. But they were also navigating a world trying to rebuild after the financial crisis and, all of a sudden, the career prospects they'd dreamed of years ago no longer made sense. "It felt like seeing the writing on the wall and thinking, 'Oh God, if things keep going down the track they're on right now, what would that look like? What would my job be?'" says Erica. Feeling at a crossroads, it was inside their friendship that they found a solution to their uncertainty.

In 2010, Claire and Erica launched Of a Kind, a much-loved ecommerce store that not only sold everything from fashion to homewares, but helped designers and makers tell the stories of their work in their own words. It was a hit. In 2015, they sold the company to Bed, Bath & Beyond, but remained working on it until 2019, when they made the difficult decision to close up shop.

When I speak to the friends and founders, I'm curious to know how they decided to continue working together after closing Of a Kind. What was that conversation like? Claire tells me that the decision to stick together was made years earlier, when the company was going through a dark time. "We'd had a meeting near my apartment and were feeling so low. We went back to my place and lay on my bed," she says. "And we were like, 'What would we want to do if we shut down? What can *we* do?' It was very clear, the only answer we wanted to figure out was how to work together. That was the most important thing."

And so they did. Since closing Of a Kind, Erica and Claire have grown their podcast and newsletter and have started a consulting company. They've also coauthored a book, *Work Wife: The Power of Female Friendship to Drive Successful Businesses*.[15] During our conversation, many of the benefits of starting a business with a friend become clear. They understand what's constantly going on in each other's lives and can empathize when that bleeds into work. They can offer a level of emotional support that would probably be strange coming from any other coworker. But they also acknowledge how rare it is to be so in the weeds of someone else's life when you're not in a romantic relationship, especially when it comes to finances. This phenomenon of going from friends to business partners with deep financial ties is something Erica and Claire explore in their book. "There's something unique about the particular strain of non-romantic partnership that we're in with each other—one that's so deeply entwined in love, taxes and other practical matters that it requires shared bank accounts, a legally binding document and a couples counsellor," they write. There may be no guidelines or contracts for friendship, but there are plenty of contracts in business, especially when your future success is as dependent on your friend as it is on your own instincts.

Claire tells me it was never an active decision to start a business with a friend. Rather, there's nobody else in the world she would want to go into business with, except Erica, who feels the same. Knowing each other intimately as friends meant they've been able to avoid many of the downfalls they've witnessed in other business partnerships, which seem to come undone when there is competition between founders. The lack of competition in their friendship, and their deep trust in each other, as well as the work ethic they both witnessed in one another back in their college days, meant that Claire and Erica were able to found their first business already knowing they'd likely be able to avoid many of the pitfalls other cofounders find themselves in. For all these years, it's their friendship that has helped their careers stay secure.

The accelerated intimacy of the workplace

Beyond the five years I spent working in retail—and the few months I spent working as a "sandwich artist" before being unceremoniously fired at the age of fourteen—I've always worked in an office. My work friendships have been made over sad desk lunches, near-constant Slack DMs, and warm glasses of cheap white wine served at 4 PM on a Friday. But every job comes with the potential for friendship.

Tilly Lawless is a queer sex worker who started working in Australian massage parlors more than ten years ago. When we speak, Tilly tells me she now works primarily in brothels, which she prefers to working privately. In the brothel, she's not responsible for her own advertising or space. She just shows up and works her shift, as she would in any other job. And like many other workplaces, there's a manager, receptionist, and anywhere between five and twenty other women: her coworkers.

When Tilly and I connect to speak about her friendships at work, the conversations and situations she describes all take place in what she refers to as the girls' room. "The vibe of the girls' room dictates the entire vibe of the establishment, because you're actually spending more time there than you are in actual bookings with clients," she tells me. "If you have an eight-hour shift, you probably spend three hours with clients and five hours with the girls, so it really matters who you're on shifts with, colleagues-wise." Inside the room there can be lounges, a kitchenette, and a number of mirrors, which create small stations for the women to do their makeup and hair while getting ready to meet clients. When Tilly first started working in brothels, there would often be a TV switched on in one corner, but these days, she tells me, most women bring their own laptop along. The vibe of the girls' room at night is more raucous, but in the daytime, Tilly, who is the author of the novel *Nothing But My Body*,[16] says she's more likely to keep to herself, reading a book or writing.

"Accelerated intimacy" is a term Tilly often uses when talking about the girls' room. "Often it's quite small and in others it's fucking tiny. You'll have three girls on one couch, three on another, and two girls shoved into the one armchair," she says. "So, you get to know each other very fast."

For a lot of women in the industry, their coworkers are the only people who know what they do for work. And it's not uncommon for women to withhold their real names from their coworkers in an attempt to separate their work life from their private life. Tilly tells me that many of the women she's worked alongside have children and partners who don't know what they do for work, so drawing boundaries between their work and personal life becomes a key to maintaining their privacy. Despite this, the joy, nurturing, and comfort of friendships are still possible.

"There's a real solidarity in the girls' room, a real feeling of support and protection," Tilly says. "But you can know so much about these people and have such an insight into their life through this accelerated intimacy, then they'll just disappear." Tilly tells me it's not uncommon to completely lose touch with someone if they decide to leave an establishment. If you're lucky, you'll run into a former friend years later, working somewhere new.

All friendship, of course, can be both situational and temporary, while still being real and impactful. A work friendship doesn't need to blend into your personal life to be meaningful, just as you don't need to be privy to coworkers' lives outside work to be able to appreciate them in the workplace.

Once, during a shift, Tilly noticed one of her colleagues in the girls' room crying after a booking with a difficult client. With a language barrier between them, Tilly simply placed a glass of water by the woman, hoping to offer what tenderness and care she could without using words. A few months later, Tilly found herself upset after seeing a different client. Within moments, the same woman placed a glass of water beside Tilly—a sign that her gesture months earlier had been seen, appreciated and was now being reciprocated. "That was so special to me, because we'd never spoken but we'd been able to develop a friendship—or a care or trust—between us anyway," she tells me. "It's a really beautiful thing to have this kind of intimacy, and we should all treasure it, regardless of whether or not it's going to be long-lasting."

When I speak to Rachel Morrison, PhD, an associate professor of management at the Auckland University of Technology who specializes in interpersonal relationships in the workplace, she tells me that there is often a single moment or event that transforms friendly colleagues into actual friends.

"There's an idea that most people can identify a tipping point—an event, day, or conversation—where they've realized that what they previously thought to be a collegial relationship has crossed the line to being a genuine friendship," she says. In an instant, I can bring so many to mind. When I found myself leaving the magazine office at the same time as my coworker, Julia, and we walked to the train together, opening up about who we were each very casually dating at the time, I knew it was the beginning of *something*. Years later, when I walked out of a New York office building for the last time after being laid off, carrying my desk plant in a cardboard box alongside Terri, Tom, and Rachel, I felt the same kind of seismic shift. Whether you're working through messy company restructures, dealing with bad clients, waiting for a delayed flight, or being quite literally stranded on an island together, there are a million opportunities for work connections to tip forward and dive headfirst into friendship outside of the workplace. "Once you have passed that tipping point, the friendship will always be different," says Morrison. I know this to be true, because it has been for me.

While I once imagined I'd be a high-flying career woman into my late sixties, I'm now sure I'd much rather retire as soon as I'm financially able (if that will ever even be possible). I'm not lazy or tired or failing, I just have a different understanding of where I find joy and meaning. I now know that when I find happiness at work, it's less likely to come from a new job title or pay raise or free lunch than from the people I'm spending eight hours a day working alongside.

When we speak about work—our relationship to it and the relationships that exist within it—everyone has a different experience to share. However, the one consistent truth I have found in my years of having friends in the workplace, and speaking to people about their own, is that work friendships are what can make all the difference between quitting and staying, failing and succeeding, admitting defeat and finding a solution. While we wait for society to be better and fairer, leaning on our friends is our best chance to make it all, well, work.

8

Breakups and Breakdowns

The only time I've considered getting a tattoo was in 2015 on New Year's Eve. I was at a party in the middle of the rainforest and a friend of a friend was sitting opposite a line of people, all patiently waiting for stick-and-pokes tattoos. "We should get matching ones," Bess said to me from the middle of the dance floor. "Even just a dot on the bottom of our feet."

In the early hours of the New Year, surrounded by strobe lights and smoke, we floated the idea of getting, somewhere on our bodies, three dots in the shape of a triangle: the symbol for infinity—a perfect representation of our decades-long friendship. It wasn't until we woke the next morning that we remembered that a dotted triangle is actually the mathematical symbol for *therefore*, not infinity. We laughed, thankful that the ink had run out before it had been our turn.

The thing about tattoos, much like close friendships, is that they're supposed to last "forever." Just as most people don't go into a tattoo parlor anticipating the painful bite of a laser-removal machine in years to come, we rarely dive into our friendships expecting they will ever come to an end. The anxieties that might coincide with the decision to get a romantic partner's name or initials tattooed on your body aren't there when it comes to similarly grand declarations of friendship. But should they be?

For a culture obsessed with romantic breakups, the experience of friendship breakdowns still feels somewhat overlooked. Despite all the art, music, films, and literature that depict the suffering of lost love, very little of it explores the specific pain of losing a close friend. Growing up, we're led to assume that losing a romantic partner trumps all other heartache. But that's not necessarily the case.

When I sit down to speak to Estelle* about the most painful breakup of her life, she still has a tattoo and somewhere, her former best friend, Holly,* has the same. As far as she knows, anyway. They haven't spoken in years.

"I didn't think twice about it," Estelle tells me, motioning toward the tattoo. "It kind of felt radical to commit in that way to someone. It felt like we were saying: Your forever person doesn't need to be family or a partner—it can be a friend."

Holly and Estelle went to high school together but didn't become close until the end of college. They were, as Estelle puts it, obsessed with each other. They would buy flowers and write poems for each other at a time when they were both setting boundaries with their families, creating space so they could figure out who they were. While they tried not to appear too desperate or clingy to the people they were dating, they relished the fact they didn't need to hide the adoration they had for each other. The tattoos, Estelle tells me, were an ode to how much they cared for each other—a forever decision for a forever friendship. But not everything can last that long.

"It is hard to recall the moment when the friendship began to unravel, but I guess the simplest way to put it is that some of our worst qualities, which had never disrupted our friendship, began to," says Estelle.

Holly had always been someone who lied a lot—about texts that "never came through," why she had to skip plans, and arguments she'd had with people that very clearly never happened—but the lies were never about anything serious, until they were. Over a period of months, the misgivings seemed to snowball, and Estelle realized that she wasn't exempt from Holly's dishonesty as she had once thought she was. "It completely undermined my sense of reality," she tells me.

Anticipating a friend's needs is a huge part of close friendship, and Holly had a lot. She lived with chronic health issues and mental health concerns, but for every problem that arose, Estelle worked to find her friend a solution—getting Holly safe and well became their shared project. It was something Estelle prided herself on, proof that she was as good a friend as she always hoped to be. When their friendship went into a tailspin, it wasn't just the loss of the relationship Estelle began to mourn, it was also her belief that friendship was the thing she was best at.

"It shook my sense of self," says Estelle. "I'm from a really dysfunctional family and my romantic relationships have never been the most important ones in my life, but I knew I was a good friend. I couldn't believe I had failed at something I'd dedicated so much of myself to."

When her friendship with Holly finally came to an end—with a final farewell text and an unfollowing spree on social media—two things surprised Estelle most. First, that the breakup had happened at all. While every married couple knows that divorce is a statistically possible ending, this was a relationship breakdown Estelle never saw coming. Second, there was the shame. The slow-growing rot that had poisoned their friendship was obvious to Estelle by the end, but that didn't make it any easier to talk about, especially to their mutual friends. There were no breakup songs to listen to, no clichéd self-care checklists to work through on her road to emotional recovery, no script to explain why they parted ways. She just had to sit with the pain.

Years after the fact, Estelle tells me the inadequacy she felt after her friendship breakup took a long time to shake.

The paranoia that she was a bad friend followed her, causing her to overcompensate in other friendships in a way she's embarrassed about now. For a long time, she regretted the care and effort she put into Holly, though she tells me she doesn't anymore. "You have to own the love and time you give to people, and I do own it now."

When I ask Estelle if she can ever see herself making up with Holly, her answer is quick. It's something she's clearly thought deeply about. "Definitely not," she tells me. "I don't wish her any suffering, but I respect myself too much."

Estelle was the first person I spoke to who was honest about the pain of a close friendship ending, but she was far from the last.

Friendship breakups feel different (because they are)

Friendships, like many of life's most precious things, are fragile. Sometimes you can see them coming to an explosive end, as stunning as that moment between dropping a glass and hearing it hit the floor. But other times, the ending is quieter, creeping up so softly that you barely notice its arrival until you look around and realize that the friend you just felt by your side has slipped out of sight. It's hard to say which kind of ending is worse.

In her memoir *True Friends*,[1] Patti Miller writes that there is a peculiar pain to realizing that you no longer matter to a friend and not knowing why—a humiliating sting. "If you don't know why lightning strikes, why a child dies, why a friend leaves, then it feels like life could—and will—give you a random smack in the teeth whenever it wants to," she writes. "Show me how one event, one action, causes the next one. Step by step. Maybe that way I can keep myself safe."

To give friendships—and friendship breakups—the weight they deserve, we often compare them to romantic relationships. But when it comes to breakups, the difference between the two doesn't necessarily lie in what we might assume: that people are sadder to lose a partner because it challenges what they believe about true love or how they imagined their future unfolding. Or that it might involve divorce, kids, or splitting assets. Of course, all those things come into play. But there's also a fundamental difference in the way we handle problems in the two kinds of relationships, which can seriously alter how they come to an end.

In 2018, researchers Cheryl Harasymchuk and Beverley Fehr looked to determine the differences between how people approach problems in their romantic relationships compared to their friendships. In their study titled "Responses to dissatisfaction in friendships and romantic relationships: An interpersonal script analysis,"[2] they found that while people expected their partner to respond to problems in an active manner—in a positive way, by engaging in a conversation about whatever was going on, or in a negative way, by getting into a huge fight about it—people were much more likely to take a passive approach to their friendships.

According to the research, when we have issues with our friends, we're likely to take one of two approaches: we either wait it out and hope that things improve without anyone actually bringing the problem up, or we withdraw from the relationship, ignore our friend, and hope they get the hint; essentially, we ghost. The concept of ghosting may have been born out of modern dating experiences but it can also haunt lost friendships.

I know the feeling of texting a friend and getting no reply, when that person used to be someone you spoke to every day, who used to send you compliments and buttery-sweet "I'm thinking of you" messages out of the blue. What I've always found most confronting about these situations is the long-lasting emotional impact they can have on you, as the faces of former friends haunt your dreams and your phone's camera roll.

It's embarrassing to tell someone you're upset because a friend won't reply to your texts, especially when that someone is also friends with the person who seems to have unsaved your number. Hearing that person's name come up in conversation—which you will—can feel like pressing on a bruise.

When dating, even if you never really know why somebody ghosted or stopped making plans with you, it can be easy to find comfort in imagining explanations. They've been so busy at work! They probably got back with their ex! They might have lost their phone! They must have moved to a new country to start a new life! Even if none of those things is remotely true, the likelihood is that you'll never really know what happened. Eventually, it becomes easier to accept that they mustn't have been that interested in you.

But when it comes to being ghosted by a friend, these theoretical excuses are harder to find. They'd just tell you if they were too busy at work to catch up; you know they haven't lost their phone because you can see they've been on WhatsApp; and if they moved to a new country to start a new life, someone sure as hell would have mentioned it to you by now. And matters only get worse when you hear that the person ghosting you has been catching up with your mutual friends, answering *their* texts, or planning long weekends away with them when that's something you've done together in the past. If you're ghosted by a date, it's fair to assume that you're not dating anymore. But everything's a little foggier when it's a friend canceling the plans. I have friends I haven't hung out with one-on-one in years, but there's no way I would stop calling them a friend, even if I didn't see them for another decade. Or even two. Still, if you go from being in near-constant contact with a close friend, making plans, confiding in one another, and something shifts, how long do you have until you can safely say the friendship is over? How do you ever know if they've called it on their end if you never speak again?

In an interview with *Time*,[3] Marni Feuerman, author of *Ghosted and Breadcrumbed: Stop Falling for Unavailable Men and Get Smart about Healthy* Relationships,[4] explained there's a key difference between friendship and romantic breakups that make the former worse. "The expectations are different in a romantic relationship," she told the magazine. "People declare themselves 'a couple,' or the relationship is very defined: we're dating, we're engaged, we're married."

Without official labels or contracts, it's easy for a friendship to silently drift so far into the distance that it becomes an invisible speck on the horizon, a memory of a friendship that once was. The pain of being ghosted by a friend isn't just difficult because of the loss it represents but also because it can feel impossible to put words to.

Unless you're in an open or polyamorous relationship, one of the key differences between friends and romantic partners is that you can theoretically have as many friendships as you want. For this reason, having an imperfect friendship, so long as it is still delivering some joy to your life, can still make sense. Friendship drift doesn't always have to end with a relationship being completely over. Sometimes, it can simply mean you're not as close to someone as you once were, without being totally out of touch. Often, only time will tell.

For every person who has been ghosted by a friend, there is someone who has done the ghosting. But if you've ever let a friendship fizzle out, it's likely that there was never a single moment when a decision to ghost was actively made. Instead, it's more likely you simply allowed a friend to drift away slowly because you felt it was for the best. Or maybe you didn't even notice it was happening.

Within my own circle, once I start asking people about friendship drift, it seems like everyone has a story. A friend tells me about the choice he made to slowly distance himself from a group of old friends who started dealing drugs. I hear from someone who had a years-long friendship drift apart after discovering their differing political preferences. In the span of a few months, I listen to at least four different stories that all involve an early-twenties trip to Europe that changed the dynamics of a friendship forever.

C. S. Lewis wrote that friendship must be *about* something, "even if it were only an enthusiasm for dominoes or white mice."[5] While the "something" our friendships are centered around might not be as obvious as a shared hobby or interest (does anyone like white mice that much?), there is usually a shared circumstance or value that keeps us bound to people in our life.

As much as I know what Lewis wrote to be true, I also know how it feels when those shared somethings begin to shift: when you realize you don't like partying as much as you once did and feel conflicted making plans with friends who still expect you to stay out until 2 AM; when a friend gets a big promotion and you have a conversation that makes you realize your values around work and money no longer align; or when someone has a baby and, for reasons you can understand on a logical and practical level, doesn't have the energy to check in and see how you're doing with your far less significant (but still very real) problems.

If I take the emotion out of these scenarios, I can consider each experience from two different points of view. For every person I spoke to who had been ghosted by a friend without warning, there was someone on the other end who had, somewhere along the way, withdrawn their attention and affection. Comparing stories of friendship drift to breakups highlights the differences those researchers discovered about our differing approaches to conflicts in these two kinds of relationships.

Friendship drift and the real problem with ghosting

When I speak to friendship coach Danielle Bayard Jackson about friendship breakups, she tells me her views on friendship drift have changed in recent years. "Honestly, I used to say that if you're trying to end a friendship you should always tell people," she says. "But now I've seen that if a friendship fizzle is mutual, it can be healthy." If both people are making less effort, she now believes it can be an easy way to mutually accept that a friendship doesn't look the way it once did. The issue arises, however, when only one person understands a drift is happening. After all, ghosting someone feels very different from being ghosted.

It can be difficult to get people to open up about their decision to let a friendship fall by the wayside. But when I speak to Ximena Angulo, I'm surprised (and grateful) that the story she wants to share with me is one in which she openly admits to ghosting a good friend. Ximena and Maria* were friends for four years, after being introduced through mutual friends. Throughout their friendship, they lived in different

countries, with Ximena in Panama and Maria in Venezuela, where Ximena was born. Despite the physical distance
between them, they were extremely close. They were vulnerable with each other, shared their dreams for the future,
and spoke every day. During their friendship, Maria came to
visit Ximena in Panama three times, staying with Ximena at
her family home. The first two trips were fun, affirming, and
memorable. But the third saw their friendship fall apart.

"I don't know what was going on in her mind or her life,
but something was different," Ximena tells me. "She seemed
bitter, but in a very subtle way that would only have been
noticeable to someone who really knew her. She criticized
many things, like my home's Wi-Fi connection, the movie my
friends chose to watch, and the way I spoke to my then-boy-
friend after he made a joke that was inappropriate." Maria
was rude to Ximena's eight-year-old sister, to the point that
Ximena's mother asked if there was somewhere else Maria
could stay. On their final night together, Maria had promised
to take Ximena and another friend out to dinner as a thank-
you for having her, but when the bill came, she gestured to
Ximena and asked if she'd be paying with cash or card, after
offering to pay for the meal of the other friend who had
hosted her. It felt like a slap in the face.

After Maria returned to Venezuela, Ximena stopped initi-
ating conversations with her. If Maria texted, she'd respond—
at first. When Maria asked what was going on, Ximena took a
passive approach, insisting everything was fine, but she eventually stopped replying completely; she ghosted her.

A year later, Ximena received a scathing email from Maria, listing the ways she'd hurt, disappointed, and been cruel to her. It was the kind of email I think many people who have been abandoned by a friend imagine themselves writing with furious taps on a laptop keyboard—the kind of email you draft in your Notes app, just in case you ever get the courage to send it.

Ximena tells me she wasn't offended by the email, even though many of her friends were on her behalf. Instead, she just felt awful. Yes, Maria had behaved badly. She had been rude and hurtful, most likely on purpose. But Ximena could have told her how she'd felt. "It might not have fixed anything, but at least she could have had closure" says Ximena. "Our friendship deserved that, and she did as well. After the email, I felt sad every time her name crossed my mind. I didn't miss her, but I felt sorry for the way things ended."

Ximena tells me the main lesson she learned through everything with Maria was that sometimes, people don't ghost their friends because they intentionally want to hurt them. She believes it's because they don't know how to be honest. "It's in that space of silence and omission, of sweeping things under the rug and looking the other way, where friendships can get lost," she says.

We don't always fight for our friendships the way we might fight for a romantic partner or work to repair a broken relationship with one of our parents or siblings. And when we sidestep our chance to take an active route, to talk it out, and see what bridge can be rebuilt, we're telling ourselves that a friendship isn't worth the effort—even when we might come to realize, years later, that it was. Even in cases when a friendship still draws to a close after talking out the problems at hand, it can be the difference between things ending respectfully or not.

The biggest of breakups

If the pain of friendship drift is unique because of its subtlety, other friendship breakups—the big, messy, dramatic ones—are painful because of the unexpected explosion they cause, blowing up your life in such a way that the ripples of their impact can be felt for years.

When I sit down with my friend Tahlia, I'm asking her to retell a story I've already heard. When we first met at work, she'd already been dating her boyfriend Liam* for a couple of years. They'd connected on Tinder, before meeting a serious partner on a dating app was common, and were now living together. It wasn't love at first sight, Tahlia tells me, but for the first few years of their relationship, she and Liam were really, truly happy. But after moving from their apartment into a house they shared with a friend, Ben, their relationship started its slow descent. They stopped going on dates, stopped being intimate. Basically, they stopped connecting in any meaningful way.

For Tahlia, her relationship with Liam ending after almost four years together wasn't exactly a surprise. Instead, it was the way it unfolded, and the involvement of someone she considered a close friend, that's been the hardest thing to get over. This detail of the breakup is why, when I was living overseas, I would often check the time in Sydney before replying to a message from Tahlia, understanding that because of the time difference, I was likely her only friend who was awake. During those sleepless hours after her breakup, I was thankful that, while I was far away, I could be there when the rest of the southern hemisphere was sleeping. Sometimes, when you can't offer a solution to a friend's hurt, all you can do is listen.

Tahlia and Zoe's* friendship started on Twitter, before they eventually met in person at a gig through mutual friends. They liked the same TV shows, the same music, and decided they should catch up again, just the two of them. They quickly became friends. "I was pretty unhappy in my relationship at that point— not that she necessarily knew that right away—but having this fun new friend was a really nice distraction," says Tahlia.

As she and Zoe grew closer, they spoke almost every day and went out together to drink and dance most weekends. Their friendship was light, easy, and fun. "We were almost in that stage of dating where you're in the honeymoon period. We were drinking a lot together, so we ended up telling each other a lot about our lives," Tahlia tells me. "I felt close to her because I was confiding in her." Zoe was never judgmental; she was understanding. Zoe made Tahlia feel like, even if she was single again in the foreseeable future, she wouldn't really be alone.

Liam had never paid much attention to Tahlia's friends—even those she'd known for years. So, when he showed an interest in Zoe, joining them for pre-dinner drinks at home a couple of times, Tahlia was grateful. Finally, her boyfriend was making an effort. But Liam's sudden interest in Zoe wasn't noticeable only to Tahlia. In fact, Zoe was the one to bring it up.

"A couple of weeks before everything came crashing down, Zoe asked me if I found it weird that Liam liked all her tweets and her photos," Tahlia remembers. She'd never really thought about it. Her main concern, now that it had been raised, was that her boyfriend was making her friend uncomfortable. "I was so ready to pick my friend over my boyfriend," says Tahlia. "I was ready to put that man in his place if he was making her feel like shit or get creeped out." But Zoe insisted it was all fine—no big deal at all—and it was left there.

A few weekends later, on a Sunday night, Zoe went over to Tahlia's place. They drank a couple of bottles of rosé and ordered pizza. Liam and Ben eventually came home, and the four of them stayed up, still drinking and picking over cold slices. As it got late, Tahlia decided to call it a night—she had to work the following morning—so she announced that she was going to bed, expecting that Zoe would head home. But she stayed. It wasn't until Tahlia heard Ben go into his bedroom about an hour later that she grew uneasy. "I was just lying there and feeling like every single puzzle piece was falling into place," she tells me. The weekend before, she'd been out and had a huge fight with Liam on the dance floor. When she went home in tears, Zoe had stayed out with the boys.

Tahlia got out of bed, and by the time she reached the bottom of the stairs she could see Liam and Zoe on the couch, sitting close under a blanket. Zoe looked like she was asleep, while Liam sat facing the muted TV. By the time Tahlia had gone to the bathroom and come back, Zoe had managed to wake up, grab her stuff, and leave without a goodbye. Liam was left sitting on the couch alone.

In a state of shock, Tahlia didn't know how to reply when Liam turned and told her that he "couldn't do this anymore." He was breaking up with her. After months of fights and promises to try and make it work, something had apparently shifted that evening.

When you hear about someone's romantic breakup—especially the sudden ones that happen within seemingly happy relationships—it's normal to be surprised, if not a little rattled. But the shock usually subsides when you hear more details or come to understand more about the couple's particular situation. When I ask Tahlia what happened next between her and Zoe, I already know the answer, but I need to hear it again. Because I've never quite gotten over it.

"Oh, that was it," she says. "I haven't seen her since that moment she was pretending to be asleep on my couch." I remember Tahlia sending me a screenshot of the Instagram post Zoe tagged Liam in, at a bar, just three days later. I remember her telling me that the day after she'd moved out, she drove past the house and saw Zoe's car parked out front.

I will never forget that just a few weeks later, Zoe met Liam's parents on a weekend trip to the Hunter Valley that Tahlia was meant to go on—the photos were plastered all over Facebook. I'll always remember the relief when they moved to another state together, and neither Tahlia nor any of her close friends had to worry about running into them on the street.

I ask Tahlia if there is a difference between being betrayed by a boyfriend and by a close friend. "It's complex," she tells me. "I don't think you can 'steal' someone's boyfriend, and I've never wanted to be that person who blames a woman, because I know Liam had a lot of ownership of that situation. But I just felt so fooled by this girl. She knew so much about me, my life, my relationship—and she still did this to me, then never spoke to me again. It felt like a blindside much bigger than a breakup."

Dr. Hannah Korrel is a neuropsychologist and the author of *How to Break Up with Friends: From Friendsh*t to Friend-split*.[6] When we speak, I'm eager to find out why some friends behave so badly that they deserve to be broken up with.

"Sometimes we forget that everyone's doing the best they can, based on the information they had at the time," says Dr. Korrel. While there's no excuse for some people's bad behavior, especially when it verges on extreme levels of mistreatment and abuse, Dr. Korrel is a proponent of showing grace to the friends who have harmed us. This grace doesn't mean welcoming them back into our lives—or even speaking to them again—but it means accepting that this person likely didn't hurt you on purpose. "You know, I'm a neuropsychologist and I have never, not once, met a psycho-path," she tells me. "It is really so rare that someone deliber-ately seeks to cause harm or maliciously hurt other people. Most people are just trying to survive."

According to Dr. Korrel, when dealing with a bad friend, it's worth looking inward at what the situation can tell us about ourselves and the behaviors we're in control of, rather than wasting energy searching for an explanation as to why a friend treated us so poorly. Since her simultaneous breakups, Tahlia has been a little more wary of new people coming into her life. With new friends—especially those who seem most interested in going out together, drinking, and only having fun—she tries to set boundaries that keep the friendships from intensifying faster than they normally would.

"What I've realized is that my friendships need to grow over time," Tahlia tells me. While we often associate the intensity of friendship with the kind of connection that makes us feel like we'd be lost without a friend, that same ferocity means a friendship can be just as capable of inflicting an unexpected amount of pain.

The unexpected pain of ambivalence

When I speak with friendship coach Danielle Bayard Jackson about friend breakups, she mentions a type of relationship that plants itself deeply in my mind: ambivalent friendships. For those who, like me, are new to the concept, an ambivalent friend is one who is simultaneously the best and the worst.

While it's easy to think of bad friends as those who are unnecessarily cruel or obviously "toxic," some of the most complicated friendships I've had in my life have been shrouded in ambivalence. These are friends who you'll either have the most fun or the most stressful night of your life with; the ones who will either celebrate your good news as if it were their own or find a way to subtly bring you down; the kind of people you can never really figure out if you love or loathe.

While some friendship breakdowns, like Tahlia's, involve an unforgivable action or decision, they are not always so straightforward. Ambivalent friendships can have their good moments, but the uncertainty they cause can make them even more detrimental to our mental and physical health than the tensions we might have with someone we'd confidently refer to as an enemy.

A study titled "Social stressors and cardiovascular response: Influence of ambivalent relationships and behavioral ambivalence"[7] found that ambivalent friendships can have a detrimental effect on our health, including our heart rate reactivity and anxiety levels.

So why do we let these friendships that mess with us so intensely stay in our lives? "The reasons we stay in relationships with people who bring us nothing can be varied," Dr. Korrel explains. "They're varied and can tap into different parts of our psyche. It might be that you were treated poorly when you were younger; that some very important people in your life made you feel like you weren't important." Dr. Korrel tells me that figuring out the "why" behind our reluctance to end bad friendships can be powerful and is best worked on with a psychologist. "You want to ask yourself, 'Why did I let that person treat me like that? Why did I stay in a relationship where I gave so much and got nothing in return?'"

But doing this kind of work isn't always easy. Dr. Korrel tells me that, especially when we're younger, we all seek out familiarity, whether it's good or bad. This makes it easy for some people to fall into patterns of welcoming the same kinds of people into their lives again and again, and being treated badly again and again. She addresses this in the work she does with her clients, but even asking yourself, "Why do I keep finding myself in this situation?" can be a helpful starting point before you decide whether you may need the help of a mental health practitioner.

When it comes to letting go of ambivalent friends, Dr. Korrel believes much of the difficulty of ending a friendship comes from people's fears of being friendless. If someone is constantly letting you down and never there for you when you need them, she argues that this person is *already* not your friend, whether you make it official or not. "Keeping up the facade that you are friends by continuing to give them all of your time, money, and effort is only costing *you* time, money, and effort," she writes in her book.

If a friend isn't making you feel supported, you likely won't feel any less alone if you slowly remove the tethers that bind you. And if the good doesn't outweigh the bad, well, perhaps therein lies your answer.

Talking it all out

As much as I have wished there was a toolkit for friendship breakups, the truth is that there will never be an equation that helps anyone decide whether a friendship should come to an end or not. During my conversations with both Danielle Bayard Jackson and Dr. Hannah Korrel, two experts who believe we should protect our energy for the people who deserve it most, it always comes back to communication. Again, our collective tendency to approach friendship with the passive idea that things will either get better without any intervention or that friendship drift can solve a problem isn't doing anyone any favors.

If you're considering ending a friendship, the only thing that seems to be clear is that it's rarely right to cut anyone out of your life without some kind of communication and, if appropriate, an opportunity to right the wrongs. "We don't have couples therapy for friendship. It would be great if we did, but I don't think people take the time to rectify any, perhaps very solvable, issues before they end friendships," says Dr. Korrel.

When I ask Jackson what she believes we should all ask ourselves before making the decision to end a friendship, the first thing that comes to her mind is whether the friend on the receiving end of our breakup text—or ghosting technique—would be shocked by our actions. She tells me that she's seen a lot of people end their friendships prematurely.

We all know what it's like to be mad at a friend. Often, it's not hard to recruit a small group of others who share similar frustrations. It's easy to get your partner, friends in other circles, or siblings onside—since they have no skin in the game. You ruminate, circling back to every comment, skipped plan, interrupted sentence, and forgotten birthday until it feels as if this friendship has cast its shadow over every part of your life.

What's less easy to imagine is bringing up any of these frustrations with the person they're aimed at. Jackson tells me that she asks her clients questions like: Does your friend know you feel taken advantage of? Do they know it upsets you when they're late? Are they aware of the fact that they never ask you questions about your day when you consistently ask about theirs? For many people, myself included, even when thinking of the friends who I feel have wronged me the most, the answer to each and every one of these questions is no. "For some of us, breaking up with a friend is a way to justify our aversion to conflict resolution," Jackson tells me.

But some friendships deserve to come to an end, since there's a price we pay for keeping bad friendships alive. A 2017 study titled "Associations among relational values, support, health, and well-being across the adult lifespan"[8] used a sample of 7,481 older adults to examine the links between support and strain from family and friends with chronic illnesses such as diabetes, cancer, lung disease, coronary heart disease, psychiatric problems, arthritis, or stroke.

The research found that only friendship strain was associated with a greater number of chronic illnesses over a six- and eight-year window. "Friendship strain was among the

only predictors of chronic illnesses in later life," researchers wrote. "Friendships were very influential—when friends
were the source of strain, participants reported more chronic
illnesses; when friends were the source of support, participants were happier." In other words, the people we choose to
hold close really, really matter.

Finding acceptance

One of the emotions Dr. Korrel points to when we're talking
about the aftermath of friendship breakdowns is, once again,
shame. Specifically, it's the fear that a friendship coming to an
end means that we are, somehow, fundamentally unlikeable,
and it's a real concern. "We're worried that if we remove the
veil from ourselves and have a look, we might see something
really awful," she says.

This reaction is one I've seen people experience during
romantic breakups. And it's a scenario we've all seen play out
on television and in movies. A teary monologue about being
unlovable or the fear of dying alone has become a trope for
characters going through traumatic heartbreak. But the key
difference is that when we've been dumped by someone we
were dating, we're likely to turn to our friends and voice our
concerns: that we're not worthy of commitment, that we
might never be able to start a family, that we have lost the
value we once saw in ourselves. But when it's a friend causing us to feel these things about ourselves, it's much harder

to voice our concerns to other friends and hear that much-needed reassurance that none of the horrible things we're thinking about ourselves are true. To question one friendship can lead us to questioning all our friendships, and keeping our shame inside only helps it become more powerful.

When we shy away from conversations about the pain and complexity of friendship breakups, we diminish their importance. For us to understand how much happiness our friendships can bring to our lives, we also need to appreciate how painful it can be for them to come to an end.

This ache of friendship breakdowns is real, burning hot in our faces during difficult conversations and in our stomachs when we run into someone we used to be close to. But after so much listening and thinking, considering, and reflecting, I've come to understand that while not all friendships are forever, there are ways to make breaking up feel more okay.

9

Loved and Lost

We don't expect our friends to die. At least, not when they're young. But this doesn't stop them from slipping out of our lives, leaving us to grapple with what it means to grieve the loss of a friend.

In February 2021, Kelly Muller posted a series of photos with her best friend, Michele, to Instagram. In the pictures, Kelly and Michele were doing what many friends in their thirties do: drinking salt-rimmed margaritas, showing up at the office in matching outfits, getting ready for a wedding. But this wasn't a birthday tribute to her closest friend, it was a digital eulogy. In the caption Kelly wrote, "Losing my best friend has been the most devastating experience of my life."

Kelly was studying at university in New Zealand when she met Michele. She was working part time in retail, and Michele, who was in high school at the time, came into the store so often that Kelly eventually asked if she wanted a job. In the sixteen years that followed they did everything together: celebrating engagements, anniversaries, promotions, new jobs, along with Kelly's wedding and the birth of her two daughters. When Michele died, they were both living in Australia, working together once again, on what would become their final project. "Michele was the first person, after our families, that my husband and I called when we had our first daughter," Kelly says. "She stood beside me when I got married. After I moved to Lennox Head, she was who I used to stay with when I came to Sydney for work. When we built our home, she was the one sending pictures of what we should be doing."

Three weeks before her death, Michele had spent a week in Lennox Head with Kelly and other friends. Now, Kelly and her family retrace the steps they took with Michele on that trip almost daily, feeling her footprints along a certain path they took together toward the beach. "When you've had a friendship for so long, even though they're not physically here, there's an energy that's still around you," she tells me. Describing that week spent together, Kelly says that, though they didn't know it, they were all lucky to have that time with Michele. Very lucky. Despite everything that has happened since, there is an unwavering gratitude for her friend, for every moment and memory. As someone who has never had to say goodbye to a close friend, it's overwhelming.

When Michele died after a long battle with depression, many international borders were still closed, meaning there was no way for her family and other loved ones in Aotearoa (the Māori name for New Zealand) and her closest friends in Australia to bid farewell to her at the same time. The morning after Michele passed, Kelly flew to Sydney to be with Michele's fiancé and other friends who had gathered to help navigate the significant amount of admin that needed to be addressed. "You didn't have time to think because everybody had something they needed to bring to the table. I don't even know how to explain that experience."

In death, many of us look to religion for reassurance that the people we loved most are being cared for and have found peace. For people like Kelly, who aren't religious, tension can fill the space between your beliefs about the so-called afterlife and the reality of how it feels to have one of your most cherished people die. For even the staunchest atheist, accepting that someone, in every iteration of themselves, is no more, can feel even more unnatural than a belief in God.

"I don't believe in heaven, so I really struggled initially. I was just trying to comprehend where she was. I wanted, more than anything, for her to be okay," Kelly tells me. "You look for signs everywhere. And whether it's just your mind tricking you or whether it's actually happening, what matters most is that you feel it. I could feel her around me and I felt that she had found peace. That gave me the confidence to just take it day by day."

Without faith to provide guidance, Kelly focused, instead, on community. While she found indescribable comfort in her friends, especially those who were also in Sydney during the days following Michele's death, she was still left wanting. Though the group of friends had each other, some often felt they weren't entitled to be grieving Michele's death as deeply as they were because they weren't technically family. Looking for reassurance, Kelly searched Instagram for hashtags like #bereavedfriends in the hope of finding someone outside her immediate circle who'd gone through what she had, but she couldn't find anything. The lack of discourse around the experience of grieving a friend's death left her short-changed in a way she wouldn't have been were she looking for a support group for people who had lost parents, partners, or children. But this shortcoming wasn't exclusive to Instagram, or social media, or even support groups. It is reflective of a society-wide gap in care when it comes to people who have lost their closest friends forever.

What we really lose when we lose a friend

In their 2019 study "Death of a close friend: Short and long-term impacts on physical, psychological and social well-being,"[1] researchers Wai-Man Liu, Liz Forbat, and Katrina Anderson wanted to understand why the grief of losing a friend wasn't taken seriously by employers, doctors, and others, when compared to the loss of a family member. The study found that losing a friend can be just as traumatic as losing a family member, with the health and well-being of the bereaved being acutely affected for up to four years.

Over a period of fourteen years, the researchers surveyed 26,515 people. Of this group, 9,586 had experienced the death of at least one close friend. Their data found that bereaved friends may need both physical and emotional support in the four years following the death. The study's conclusion notes that the loss of a close friend is a type of "disenfranchised grief," rendering a significant impact on people's mental and physical health, vitality, and social functioning. The study also found that bereaved women in particular experienced "more negative and long-lasting" outcomes after this kind of loss.

When I Zoom with Dr. Forbat from Australia to her home in Scotland, she describes vitality as "engagement in life." Suddenly, the term's inclusion in this research feels particularly painful when we talk about the repercussions of someone's death, as if, in one person's death, there are many lives at least momentarily lost. The phrase "I couldn't live without you" takes on new meaning.

"There's this really unhelpful discourse around bereavement where the first year is hard, but from there everything is easier because you've done the first birthday and first anniversary of someone's death, along with any religious or cultural traditions," she says. "But we know that's not the case for everyone, whether you're a family member or not."

In her research and practice as a family therapist, Dr. Forbat is passionate about challenging the hierarchy of grief, which places someone's biological family at the top of the pyramid, with all other relationships falling below it. Instead of "close friends," Dr. Forbat often uses the phrase "psycho-logical kin" to refer to the people we choose to be close to, sometimes over and above our biological family.

Having worked in palliative care and cancer research for decades, she's seen firsthand how psychological kin—our friends—are neglected by institutions, even those like the World Health Organization, which appear to understand that both family and friends are a core element of palliative care. But despite the importance of close friendship being widely acknowledged within the medical industry, Dr. Forbat doesn't often see this put into practice. For example, many palliative care units will send a hand-written card to loved ones of the deceased two weeks after their death, then again six months later. But these acts of care are normally reserved for spouses or adult children and very rarely close friends.

For Americans between twenty-five and thirty-four, the first ranked cause of death[2] is unintentional injury, which includes poisoning and motor vehicle accidents, followed by suicide, then homicide. I ask Dr. Forbat if there's a difference in the grief we feel following the death of young people, who are more likely to die by suicide or in a car crash, than the grief we might feel for older relatives, for example, whose death is more likely to be attributed to coronary heart disease or dementia. I'm not shocked when she says there is, explain-ing that unexpected or traumatic deaths, such as suicides or sudden accidents, leave the bereaved at much higher risk of prolonged grief disorder, where the symptoms of grief persist for longer than twelve months and affect the ability to function in daily life.

In Australia, employees are entitled to two days of compassionate and bereavement leave when someone in their immediate family or household dies. By the government's definition, "immediate family" can include your spouse or former spouse, de facto partner or former de facto partner, child, parent, grandparent, grandchild, or sibling. This leave policy also extends to the immediate family of your partner or former partner, as well as step-relations and adoptive family. Of course, this kind of leave policy is vital and not to be taken for granted at a time when other countries, including the US, have no federal laws around grief, loss, or funeral arrangements. Still, it's obvious where policies like Australia's fall short.

I ask Dr. Forbat what she thinks it may take to change the way workplaces, and society at large, care for bereaved friends, and she takes a moment before answering. "The dismantling has to come from people challenging these normative ideas about who's impacted by grief. But you can only start to do that through dialogue, then through shifting policies," she says.

Dr. Forbat tells me that the previous week she'd been in a meeting at her university about Scotland's bereavement policy. In the last few years, several of her team members—herself included—had lost a parent. Their current policy was similar to Australia's, offering some paid leave to people who had lost a parent or spouse, then several fewer days for a more distant relative or friend. It was at this moment Dr. Forbat was able to put everything she's learned through her research into practice, starting a conversation about the grief hierarchy within the group.

"These policies need deconstructing and, maybe, if we get to dismantle them, then we won't have staff members being told they can only have one day off 'because, well, it was only your best friend of forty years who died,'" she tells me. "We need to shift the tone of this whole conversation into something that recognizes the strength of a bond, rather than some random label that's been attributed to our bio-logical kin." The university's HR representative in the room took notes.

The idea that conversations like this, taking place in small meeting rooms around the world, are what will influence long-term institutional change almost feels too optimistic. But, as Dr. Forbat points out, this is often the way policy changes become a reality.

When issues are given a certain level of visibility, it makes it easier to readjust the rules. Sometimes, you just need some evidence and some stories—you need power—and then everything flips.

Proving what you have lost

Lech Blaine was seventeen when he jumped in a car with six friends. Together, the teenage boys—five seated in the car with another two in the trunk—were making a short trip from a barbecue to the city after a lift fell through. With Lech in the front passenger seat, his friend who was driving, sober and under the speed limit, overcorrected on a bend and crossed onto the opposite side of the road, colliding with an oncoming car. The accident resulted in the death of three passengers—Will, Hamish, and Henry—and left others in induced comas and, in one case, permanently disabled. Lech was the only one to walk away from the crash unharmed. Physically, at least.

Lech, who is now in his thirties, is used to talking about the accident and his friends, though he admits to me the latter was much harder to write about. In his book, *Car Crash: A Memoir*,[3] he explores the tensions that can arise when friendship, tragedy, grief, and loss intersect—in his case, each fueled by the potency of teenage friendship. When I speak to Lech, I expect him to articulately reflect on the accident and the friends he lost in it, as he does in his book, but what I'm most curious about is how it has shaped the friendships he has built since then, as he finished school, left his hometown, went to university, and grew up. But to get to that point, I know it's vital to talk about what Lech lost on that night in May 2009.

"Friendship is such a convoluted thing, especially when you add grief to it," Lech begins, echoing a message I've heard before. The complicated nature of friendship is, at its heart, what makes these relationships so much harder to define than others, both in life and in death.

Lech's accident came at the end of a whirlwind summer. One of his friends had started at a new school that year on a football scholarship, and Lech had spent the months leading up to the crash making friends with the boys who had embraced his old friend. Together they'd formed a new group, defying the barrier of attending different high schools—something which anyone who has grown up in a small town is sure to agree can feel like a bigger deal than it ought to be. It was a glorious summer, despite the usual teenage insecurities, competitiveness, and a constant fear of being left out, but even in the perfect chasm in which it existed, there's every chance that without the accident, it could have been completely forgettable. The act of making new friends has always come naturally to Lech, even as a teenage boy, when the kind of love he expressed to his friends was hardly the norm.

"I've always had a fairly intense approach to friendship, to the point where it's noticeable to other people. When I was a teenager, then at college, people would make fun of me because I would have these romances with people I met and really liked," he tells me. "Not to be flippant, but I think the reason I was in the accident is because I'm that kind of person."

As our conversation continues, it's clear what kind of person Lech considers himself. The kind of person who meets a group of boys from a different school and gets so swept up in these new friendships that he's soon considered a vital part of the group. The kind of person who was so open to new friendships in his youth, it didn't matter that his own schoolmates thought he was a bit of a traitor having this new group of friends. The kind of person who can still look back on the season in which he lost three friends and see the beauty in a million insignificant moments.

"The thing about death, especially when it happens to someone young, is that it kind of freezes a person at a point in time. And it freezes your feelings toward them. When you experience grief, it's very easy to feel nostalgic about the people you've lost," he says.

For Lech, who was mourning his friends in 2009, social media was an unexpected comfort when trying to unknot the complicated hierarchy of grief. Of the three boys who passed away in the accident, Lech was closest to Henry, who was, much like Kelly's Michele, someone who was considered a best friend by many. After Lech learned of Henry's death, he posted a status on Facebook and changed his profile picture to one of them together. "The main emotion I felt was regret that we hadn't taken more photos," he writes in *Car Crash*. "How else could I prove what I had lost?"

Henry and Lech hadn't been friends for all that long, but their friendship was intense. As many teenage relationships did at the time, my own very much included, this private closeness became public on Myspace. At the time of the accident, Lech was Henry's third or fourth "top friend." It felt validating, he tells me, to have that reflection of their friendship suspended in time.

Top friends on social media, much like some teenage friendships in real life, could be fleeting. Now, looking back, Lech can acknowledge that while he found personal comfort

in the ranking, it could have been equally minimizing for
friends who perhaps knew Henry longer or considered him
one of their closest friends. Even with a documented friendship ranking, there was nuance to be found when it came to
determining the hierarchy of grief within the circle of Henry's many friends.

"Within the mourning process there are fairly defined
roles and hierarchies: parents and siblings, then usually a
best friend or the people who are pallbearers. But then there
are people who don't quite make that cut, who are caught
in limbo. It can be a very alienating and lonely experience
because you no longer have that person who's died there to
justify your friendship to everyone. It's gone," he says. "If
your friend dies during a time when you're not quite as close
to them, it suddenly throws your whole understanding of
your connection into flux."

Lech tells me he was talking to a friend recently, reflecting on other teenage friendships they both had, which have
faded with time. They wondered if, had Henry, Hamish, and
Will not died in the accident, they'd even be friends today.
Through the death of his friends, Lech has found himself
appreciating the millions of other ways friendships can end,
and how preferable each of those many options is to what
he went through. "It would have been such a beautiful thing
to have just been friends with these people, then drift away
from them over time," he says.

After spending so much of my life worried that my oldest
friendships will change so much they become unrecognizable,

or disappear forever, I find myself simply feeling thankful that I've never had to grapple with the finality of a friend's death. Never talking to a friend again, even if over a petty disagreement or mistake you regret, will never be worse than truly losing them.

Continuing bonds

The night following my call with Kelly, I find myself searching online for photos of chamomile, small flowers stuffed with white petals, sitting at the end of thin wriggling stems.

The year before Michele passed away, she sent Kelly a bunch of flowers for her birthday. When they arrived, Kelly opened the box to find a scraggly bunch of chamomile blooms in place of Michele's usual choice of peonies or an all-white bouquet. She texted her friend to tell her there must have been some kind of mistake with the order. "I sent her a photo and was like, 'Oh mate, they've sent me the wrong bunch, look at the state of this,'" she remembers, laughing. "She replied and told me that they were actually her new favorite flowers and that I was just doing it wrong, then sent me a photo of them in her home where she'd put them in vases with red David Austin Roses."

Now, every two weeks when chamomile flowers are in season, Kelly visits her local florist to buy them. She says that on every visit, the same florist remarks on how beautiful the flowers are, to which Kelly can never force herself to agree.

"I hate them," she says. "But I buy them, because it's her. I've even planted chamomile seeds in the garden of our new home."

Since losing Michele, Kelly has found ways to keep her in her life. When she first started writing Michele letters, they were filled with heart-aching concern and questions about where she'd gone. Now, the letters are updates on everything that has happened since she left, an intentional effort to keep the conversation between them going. When Kelly runs, which she does a lot since losing her friend, she finds herself talking to Michele out loud over the music in her headphones. She watches the sunrise as often as she can, and thinks of her every time. She keeps photos of Michele on her fridge. And on Friday afternoons, Kelly's husband makes her a margarita in one of their fancy glasses, the kind Michele had a strong preference for, and they toast to her, wherever she is.

When working to help people who have experienced loss and grief, Dr. Forbat encourages them to consider who they are now that their friend has died, along with exactly what they've lost. "You and your best friends share stories that nobody else does. You can tell someone else a story, but it's not the same as when the two of you think back and laugh or cringe," she says. "There's something really important in witnessing the loss of that connection, the loss of that intimacy and the parts of you that disappear when you no longer have the ability to talk about that story with that person. This is why loss is really hard, because you're losing someone who knew you in a very specific way, in very specific contexts."

I imagine my closest friends standing in a line, each holding one end of a makeshift telephone crafted with a piece of string and two empty tin cans. I imagine our memories running along the strings like electric currents. Bess and I having the police called on us, after dressing up in costumes and slinking along my suburban street in an attempt to scare our younger siblings. Tim and I spending a sleepless night in a train station in India, after our train from Agra to Mumbai was delayed by twelve hours.

With Dr. Forbat's words in mind, I imagine each taut string being cut with a pair of freshly sharpened scissors, leaving two frayed ends flickering as one end of our shared memories disappears forever. And it hurts. Despite existing only in my imagination, just for a moment, it's a loss that cannot be explained. There may not be a language for friendship, but every friendship has a language of its own, made up of inside jokes, secret nicknames, and invented words. This is the language we stand to lose completely when we lose a friend. Kelly's remark about Michele's chamomile flowers gets stuck in my head for weeks, but sharing the story with me will never compare to her laughing about it with Michele.

In *Boy Friends*,[4] poet Michael Pedersen somehow manages to put words to this specific pain, writing of his beloved friend Scott Hutchison, who passed away in 2018. Michael and Scott had been vacationing together in the days before Scott went missing. The days spent driving through Scotland, swimming in hotel pools, and feasting on indulgent

seafood platters left Michael on the police's list of the last
people to have seen Scott. The final time Michael saw his
friend, he was boarding the 10:10 AM train home.

Those who are familiar with Scott, the much-loved lead
singer of the band Frightened Rabbit, likely know what happened next. A number of distressing tweets from his account.
Thousands of concerned fans recalling Scott's lyrics about
his own mental health and suicidal ideation. And, a day later,
an update that Scott was gone, his body found by a kayaker.

In his memoir, Michael writes of the phenomenon Dr.
Forbat and I discussed, of countless abrupt endings to conversations and plans that were either due to be enjoyed or
were in the middle of being lived. "The ink is still wet on
the page so there's no way the book's gone up in flames," he
writes. "You can't be dead because we are still mid-conver-
sation on a hundred relatively inconsequential things, and
we're about to pick these conversations back up and finish
the suckers off like we said we would."

Much of Michael's *Boy Friends* is written *to* Scott, rather
than *for* him. In the book's prologue, he writes, "Now that
you're gone, I want to talk about you more than I care to
admit. I find ways to meander and U-bend conversations
into stories with you at the yolk of them." It's a habit I imagine Dr. Forbat would approve of.

Michael's practice of writing to Scott, much like Kelly's
ongoing conversations with Michele, are examples of a theory known as "continuing bonds." In 1996, researchers Dennis Klass, Phyllis R. Silverman, and Steven Nickman coedited

Continuing Bonds: New Understandings of Grief,[5] a book out-lining this concept, which seeks to challenge predominantly Western beliefs about the modern grief process.

The concept of continuing bonds is built around the idea that we don't have to sever all ties with people who have passed, relieving people of the expectation "to 'recover,' to 'put the past behind them,' and 'to get on with their lives.'" Instead, those who are grieving are encouraged to continue their relationship with the person who has died, albeit in a different way from when they were alive. Many people already do this, even without awareness of this model of grief. By speaking to the dead, starting new rituals or routines with them in mind, or visiting places that meant a lot to them, we are, in some way, acknowledging that our bond with someone who has died is never entirely broken or buried—it's still there. It's just taken a new shape.

Coming together through loss

It's instinctual to think of a person's family first when you hear of their death. Walking my dog on an autumn afternoon, I saw a crowd gathered at the very end of my street. Seeing a man lying on the footpath, I hurried up, my mind occupied by the idea that I could help, living so close. Maybe he just needed a glass of water or, at worst, a towel to stop any potential bleeding. From the edge of the small group, I watched someone do chest compressions on the man on the footpath, while someone else held a phone on loudspeaker within earshot. I could hear a voice on the other end of the emergency line counting out a beat.

"He's long gone," a couple who were also standing at the fringe of the group told me. So I kept walking, conscious of making as little a spectacle of this stranger's sudden death as I could.

That night, I called my mom, as I do whenever there's an unsettling feeling I can't seem to shake. I hadn't done this in years, but as soon as she answered, my voice broke and I cried over the phone. I told her I couldn't stop thinking about the man's partner, kids, family. At the time, I didn't spare a thought for his friends, despite the fact that he may have had no family or partner waiting for him at home that day. It's impossible to know who will really be affected by the loss of any person, whether they're a stranger at the end of your street, a colleague, or an acquaintance.

Kelly has considered deeply the similarities and differences between friends and family during times of loss. "Your family is your family, of course, but if you're not close with them, there's so much they don't know about you," she says. "My sister has no idea what excites me, what drives me, my favorite food, my favorite restaurants or what to buy me for Christmas." Kelly and Michele had been friends for sixteen years—they knew when the other had the day off work or a busy week coming up. It was a kind of familiarity that could never be replicated by anything other than choosing to share themselves with each other inextricably.

Another issue with the hierarchy of grief is the way it separates those who are grieving without encouraging different groups to rely on each other for support, as is the case with ring theory. The hierarchy encourages mourning people to stay separated: Family grieves with family, friends grieve with friends. But what if this weren't the case? What if we collectively understood that there really is so much to gain by looking beyond the pyramid? What if we all understood how much solace there is to be found by looking around to see who else is mourning the same person you are?

Tim Brennan was, in his sister Bella's words, the most adoring big brother. At family events, kids would hang from his limbs and follow him through houses and into backyards. The day after Bella gave birth to her daughter, he appeared at the hospital with a bag full of gifts. He was energetic, fun, and charismatic. The Verve's "Bitter Sweet Symphony" was one of his favorite songs.

Bella and Tim, along with their other two siblings, were incredibly close—a "perfect foursome"—until Tim's family lost him to alcoholism. "Tim had so much more life to live," Bella tells me. "I just keep imagining everything he should be doing, in some parallel universe."

The days after death move quickly and slowly at the same time. They can be foggy but also clarifying, as it becomes clear who else is sharing the weight of your grief. After Tim passed, his best friend, Hugh, was right there by the family's side. While Hugh's grief and Bella's grief were different, their connection has been a light in the darkest time.

"Hugh just showed up from the beginning. And he's never stopped showing up. Sometimes I just can't believe it," Bella tells me. "We know the family side of Tim, but Hugh has all the stories from high school and of them living together in their mid-twenties. We're both gatekeepers of all the pieces of Tim. When we come together it's almost like we're piecing him back together as a whole."

The day after Tim's funeral, Hugh checked his mailbox. During a pandemic lockdown, Hugh had moved into a home Tim never had the chance to visit. Still, on this particular day, a letter arrived at Hugh's place addressed to Timothy Brennan. He called Bella right away. The letter, it turned out, was a piece of political junk mail that might have, in any other instance, been thrown straight into the trash. After some investigating, it was found that a different Tim Brennan had lived in the home years before. Bella, who has never been religious, believes it was divine timing, a reminder that if Tim is looking down on them, he'd be stoked to see how his family and friends have come together. That day was the first and last time Hugh received anything for a Tim Brennan at that address.

After Tim passed, Bella looked for every reminder of him inside her phone. She reread their messages, watched family videos, and scrolled through her entire camera roll. But eventually, she exhausted every avenue and found there really was nothing left. Then came more of Tim's friends. More photos. More memories. Each one a precious gift.

"I'm in touch with friends from all different chapters of his life now," she says. "I'm always chatting to one of his work colleagues, a British guy Tim worked in recruitment with. We're constantly in touch and sometimes he'll just shoot me a memory of Tim. I never expected that. He brings a whole new perspective of what he was like at work, which I'd never been privy to seeing." Tim died in November, so when his birthday came around the following October, it was nearing the first anniversary of his death. Tim's family invited his friends to a barbecue at his dad's house, along with his close family. With the invitation came a request that everyone wear a flannel shirt: Tim's uniform. The group ate and played backyard cricket. Bella describes the day as a happy kind of funeral.

Just months after Tim passed, another one of his friends, Stu, welcomed his second baby and gave him the middle name Timothy. At the barbecue, Tim's family got to meet his namesake.

At the time of our conversation, Bella is counting down to her wedding. It's going to be a small celebration, she tells me, but it feels important to have Hugh and his wife there. "I will have my other brother James there, representing my brothers, but Hugh represents the other side to Tim," she says. As we talk about the wedding, I think of what Bella and her family stood to lose if they hadn't fully understood the depth of Tim's friendships, how they shaped him, and the influence he had on the lives of people outside his family. I think of what a missed opportunity it must be for families who are unable to look past their own grief and do the same.

A parting wish

Before Jonathan Tjarks passed away, he wrote an essay for *The Ringer*, the sports and pop culture website where he worked, headlined "Does My Son Know You?"[6] In the piece, he wrote about being diagnosed with terminal cancer, the boredom of waiting for PET scans, his faith, his family, and the relationship he had with his own father, who was diagnosed with Parkinson's disease when Jonathan was six, then died fifteen years later. Jonathan wrote that as his own death approached, he'd already told his friends the only thing he was going to ask them when he eventually saw them in heaven: "Does my son know you?"

"I don't want Jackson to have the same childhood that I did. I want him to wonder why his dad's friends always come over and shoot hoops with him. Why they always invite him to their houses. Why there are so many of them at his games. I hope that he gets sick of them," he wrote.

This was a call to action for Jonathan's friends, a request that they not only hold him in their memories but continue to play their parts as if cancer had never found its way into his body. This deep understanding of the roles our friends can fill in the lives of our family should not have felt so revolutionary to me, but such is the result of the ignorance with which we treat friendship after a death.

Because death is inevitable. No number of seat belts and safe drivers, charity fundraisers and therapy sessions, plasma infusions and blood donations can save our lives forever. And as long as no guarantee to protect our friends exists, all we can hope for is a shared understanding of exactly what we lose when we lose a friend. To truly understand the magnitude of friendship, we must sit with how it feels to have it slip away.

When I imagine my own death, should I be so lucky for it to happen when I am old, with a full life of love behind me, I hope my friends will be thought of when I pass. I hope that our closeness will have been common knowledge, and just as respected as the relationships I have with my partner, family, or children. I hope somebody asks my friends if they are okay. I hope they are fed and cared for. If they are still working, I hope, at the very least, that they are given the day off.

10

Letting Go of the One

I love asking close friends how they met. In our romantic relationships, the practice of sharing the stories of our firsts—first texts, first dates, first dances, first anniversaries—loudly, proudly, and publicly isn't just encouraged but frequently expected. However, when it comes to friendship, these memories are often left untold, sitting silent in our chests, recounted only in the occasional birthday speech or wedding toast. Beyond these rare moments, when we're granted permission to speak, we ignore our friendship love stories—even when they prove themselves to be more long-lasting and life-affirming than the relationships we have with the people we date or even marry.

Nerida Ross and Maddison Costello met in college while taking the same art history course. At the time, Nerida referred to Maddi as her "theater friend" after they fell into a habit of going to see shows together—something none of their other friends ever wanted to do. As they neared the end of their studies, they each shared that they'd been wanting to go overseas on one last big trip before starting full-time work. They decided to do it together. "I remember saying to one of my high school best friends, 'I barely know this person—we're just theater friends and we're about to go on a three-month trip together,'" Nerida tells me.

Any concerns were soon put to rest as they explored Mexico, Colombia, and Cuba. While traveling, Maddi lost her phone, then Nerida lost her passport and wallet. By the end of the trip, they were joking that they'd become two halves of one whole. With Maddi unable to contact anyone and Nerida without any money, they shared one phone and one credit card for the remainder of their trip. "We were in hostels telling people we were one whole now and everyone was like: You guys are finding this way funnier than you should be," remembers Nerida.

When they returned home, Maddi and Nerida became inseparable. They started DJing together at least twice a week and became a kind of package deal in their personal lives too—if one was invited somewhere, the other was, too. In the years that followed, it wasn't uncommon for them to arrive at a friend's dinner party and be the only non-romantic couple invited. When they started DJing weddings, weekends involved long drives and conversations—many about the strangers' weddings they'd just attended. Both working in production, Maddi and Nerida have always had a lot of opinions about event spaces, lighting, speeches, music, and catering. And most of the time, their opinions were the same. If they were ever to throw a wedding, they both agreed it would be epic.

When I ask Maddi and Nerida when they decided to throw their friend wedding, affectionately known as their "uncivil ceremony," they tell me they have different versions of how it came to be. For Maddi, it was those hundred little conversations about weddings that led them to the idea that if they hosted one, it would be perfect. For Nerida, the moment is more specific.

After losing her dad, Nerida would often find herself crying behind the DJ booth during wedding speeches, even when she didn't know the couple who were getting married. One night, following a particularly beautiful wedding of a mutual friend, Nerida tells me she went back to the accommodation she was sharing with Maddi and broke down. "I was telling her that I was just so sad, because my dad will never be at a wedding that I have," says Nerida. "I told her that, no matter what—if I get married to anybody—it will be a sad day, no matter how perfect it is. And she just said to me, 'Don't worry, we can have a wedding and it will be the best.'"

The uncivil ceremony, which was somewhere between a joke and an earnest celebration of their friendship, was held to coincide with Nerida's and Maddi's thirtieth birthdays.

Together, they planned a party of epic proportions, invit-
ing 150 family and friends to Nerida's mom's house, where
they'd laid checkered flooring, built a stage, and arranged for
a friend's seven-piece band to play. When planning the party,
both Maddi and Nerida agreed they wanted their wedding
to feel heartwarming but also be quite funny. They decided
the theme of the party would be "wedding" so that everyone could dress as a bride, bridesmaid, or wear a suit if they
wanted to. "It was really fun and subconsciously took a little
bit of the focus off us," Maddi tells me.

Nerida wore a navy-blue suit with embroidered flames on
the sleeves, while Maddi wore a strapless black dress with
opera gloves, each adorned with a giant baby-blue bow.
While there wasn't a ceremony per se, there were speeches
and a cake. As a surprise, Nerida asked her friends in the
band to write a song for Maddi, which was played early in
the night.

Falling in line with their birthdays, the wedding also happened just weeks before Nerida moved from Australia to
Canada. "With the timing, particularly for me, it actually
really felt like a public commitment," Maddi tells me. "It was
like, even though we're not going to be in the same place, I
am saying to myself and to everyone here that this is a really
important relationship that I'm going to work on and keep in
my life. It was nice to be able to do that."

But for all the joy of the wedding, it came along with its
own unique anxieties too. When they first started planning
the event, both Nerida's and Maddi's mothers expressed how

uncomfortable they were with the concept. Both progressive, feminist women, their fear wasn't that their daughters were making a commitment to each other in a romantic or queer sense—rather, it was that they seemed to be rejecting the idea of romance completely. The idea of their daughters marrying a friend, same-sex or not, wasn't anywhere near as alarming as the idea that this could mean they wouldn't marry anyone for real—for *true love*—in the future. "Our moms reacted really similarly," Maddi tells me. "I remember mine saying, 'But what if you meet someone one day and you actually want to get married to them? Do you think they might be confused that you had a wedding with Nerida?' And I was like, 'No, I think if I was going to marry someone, they would know me well enough to understand my relationship with her.'"

Despite more people choosing to reject the tradition of marriage, our romantic relationships are still at the center of modern life. Today, marriage is an automatic recognition of someone's next of kin and a right hard-fought for by members of the queer community. But the more I speak to people about their friendships, the more my feelings about the romance, intimacy, and love that we can wrap our friends in are validated.

The idea that grand acts of commitment and adoration should be saved only for those with whom we're in a sexual relationship seems more stifling the longer I think about, observe, and pay attention to the tenderness of my own friendships. While polyamory, ethical non-monogamy, and asexuality each challenge the bounds of platonic and romantic love, for the most part society still has rigid rules as to who is allowed to show love to whom.

The history of romance and friendship

It was surprising to learn that people didn't always value romance above friendship. Just as the push toward the nuclear family was fueled by capitalism, at the expense of the village, the idea that our romantic relationships should be valued above all else is one that has been influenced by society's changing values of work and community. In *The All-or-Nothing Marriage: How the Best Marriages Work*,[1] Eli J. Finkel writes about the historical shift of focus from pragmatism to love, which occurred within marriages after the Industrial Revolution. Before industrialization, people were often closest to their friends and considered marriage a relationship based on economics and security more than love and tender feelings.

"Industrialization set the stage for love's triumph—ultimately producing the breadwinner-homemaker, love-based marriage immortalized in 1950s sitcoms—by radically altering America's economy and social structure," writes Finkel. As households became richer, more suburban, and more nuclear, people felt less concern about their basic needs of safety, food, and shelter. But with this comfort came a perceived lack of need for the people who once provided the love that marriages didn't: close friends.

When society's perceptions of romantic relationships shifted, the pendulum swung so far it completely knocked over the bonds people had built and nurtured with close friends, neighbors, and their community. According to Finkel, industrialization weakened our social ties. In the US, people moved to cities, where they were less likely to make friends with neighbors. As friendship became harder to access outside the home, people looked for everything they once got from their community from their partner. As our view of marriage changed, so did our perception of friendship and its importance.

If industrialization provided fertile ground for the narrative that romantic love is the answer, Romanticism is where the idea flourished. It was during the Romantic era that people began to place an emphasis on the importance of our emotions, imagination, and the wonders of love and nature. Romanticism arrived as an antidote to the struggles of an industrialized world, but through literature, art, and music, it also created many of the ideas that still sit firmly at the heart of modern beliefs. We expect love to conquer all because we invest so much in finding it. And to give romantic love the power and gravitas society has been so convinced it deserves, we've let our friendships wither by the wayside.

The hesitation to show affection to our closest friends is something Dr. Marisa G. Franco writes about in her book *Platonic: How the Science of Attachment Can Help You Make—and Keep—Friends*.[2] "We are petrified to express love for our friends because if we do, we risk accusations of being attracted to them," she writes. "But this muddling reveals our collective confusion as to different forms of love."

Of course, what Dr. Franco is really touching on is how the influence of homophobia and heteronormativity on our friendships, particularly evident in the lack of a label for close male friends (*boyfriends*, unlike *girlfriends*, isn't typically used to refer to platonic relationships), has created a hesitation to show physical affection to people we wouldn't want to appear sexually attracted to. And while the acceptance of different sexualities and gender identities has made great progress in the last decades, who we feel we're *allowed* to be close to is still affected by heteronormativity.

In *Platonic*, Dr. Franco references Angela Chen, the author of *Ace: What Asexuality Reveals about Desire, Society, and the Meaning of Sex*,[3] who says there are three types of love—platonic, romantic, and sexual—which can overlap or be felt separately. Before marriage and romantic love became so intertwined, people were more likely to feel romantically about their friends, and show them types of nonsexual affection, like holding hands, which is now usually reserved for whoever we're dating. "Romantic love in friendship isn't radical," writes Franco. "When we pretend romantic love is abnormal in friendship, we leave people ashamed and confused by the deep love they feel for friends. Then, instead of expressing this love, they bury it."

When I speak to people about their closest friendships, love is the undercurrent of every conversation. The more we love our friends, the more they can frustrate, inspire, or disappoint us. The love we feel for our very best friends may be different from the love we feel for a partner, but that doesn't mean it's any less real or any less important. And when partners feel threatened by this love, it's due to the misunderstanding that different kinds of love can coexist. So why is the love we have for these people consistently placed second to romantic love? Why do we focus so much on finding *the one* when there is so much love to be found and shown to our friends, who can reciprocate that love whether we're single, in a relationship, or nursing a bruised heart? If all kinds of love—platonic, romantic, sexual—are equal, and can exist independent of one another or happily overlap, perhaps it's time to reconsider how we balance the scales.

The magic of single friends

When I was in my early twenties, a year after breaking up with my first long-term boyfriend, I had a get-together with six of my closest friends to celebrate 365 days of being single. We gathered on a picnic blanket at an outdoor cinema, and I drank a tiny bottle of champagne (likely plucked from a freebie table at work) through a paper straw. A photo from that night is still on my Facebook page, posted with the painfully 2010s caption *Celebrating life with these ones.*

Though the theoretical purpose of that night was to celebrate a year of independence and a full recovery from heartbreak, looking back, it wasn't really about my romantic life—or single status—at all. While I'm sure I thought I was being extremely cryptic at the time, my Facebook caption really did say it all. I was celebrating a year of unabashed, uncomplicated, and completely life-changing friendship. Today, more than a decade later, four of those six friends in that photo are still part of my closest circle—a fact which I wholly credit to those years we spent so tightly bound.

For single women, friendship can easily be prioritized above all else. And it's magic.

In her 2016 book *All the Single Ladies: Unmarried Women and the Rise of an Independent Nation*,[4] Rebecca Traister argues that for women, single life is liberation. "Among the largely unacknowledged truths of female life is that women's primary, foundational, formative relationships are as likely to be with each other as they are with the men we've been told since childhood are supposed to be the people who complete us," she writes.

It's Traister's belief, much like that of Angela Chen, that there are many types of loving relationships, but none that should ever automatically be prioritized above another. After hundreds of interviews with single people, Traister hoped to question our definition of what counts as a "real" partnership. "Do two people have to have regular sexual contact and be driven by physical desire in order to rate as a couple? Must they bring each other regular mutual sexual satisfaction? Are they faithful to each other?" she writes. "By those measures, many heterosexual marriages wouldn't qualify."

Toward the end of my conversation with Nerida and Maddi, I'm asked if I've seen *that* episode of *Sex and the City*.

The episode, of course, is "A Woman's Right to Shoes,"[5] in which main character, Carrie Bradshaw, has a pair of Manolo Blahniks stolen at a baby shower. After her friend Kyra, who hosted the party, refuses to pay Carrie the 485 dollars the shoes were worth, Carrie calculates that in their years of friendship she's bought Kyra an engagement gift, a wedding gift, and three baby gifts, and she's traveled out of state for her wedding. In total, Carrie works out that she's spent more than 2,300 dollars celebrating Kyra's choice to get married and have kids. It's in this moment of frustration that Carrie realizes something so many single women I know relate to: There are no celebrations for explicitly single people. As Carrie puts it, "Hallmark doesn't make a congratulations-you-didn't-marry-the-wrong-guy card. And where's the flatware for going on vacation alone?"

Friendships among single women have an intensity that's both hard to describe and impossible to replicate. In a world where we're constantly told that romantic love can—and should—conquer all, the times it's easiest to give our friendships the attention they deserve often comes when we're not in a romantic relationship. When we're single, the space that could be occupied by a lover is free to be filled up by friends—not just by one, but many. With more room to evolve and become more intimate, it's a joy to see what shape a friendship can take; what it can be capable of.

Before Nerida left for Canada, she helped her mom move out of the house where the uncivil ceremony had been held. "I was helping my mum and I was thinking that if I don't ever end up having a relationship or kids, I would actually love to just be that person who is, like, fucking *there* for people when they need someone," she tells me. "If your mum dies, I will come and cook for you every single day. If you need to move, I will be there."

Maddi agrees, noting that this kind of attitude isn't necessarily an indictment against having kids or finding a long-term partner but simply a way of imagining a future where you have more resources to offer your friends than people with families do. "I think there's something really nice about being more of an independent agent, where you can give your friends all of this time," she says. "It would be good to be the person who can just turn up at a moment's notice and who potentially has more of a disposable income." And it's not just about single people being able to give friends the care they need—single people can also be most likely to need this kind of care in return.

A 2022 study titled "Differentiating the impact of family and friend social support for single mothers on parenting and internalizing symptoms"[6] looked to compare the type of support single mothers were given from family and friends. Researchers found that while both kinds of support were important, they were also quite distinct from one another. While both family and friends were able to provide parenting support, only the support of single mothers' friends resulted in fewer internalizing symptoms, like sadness, depression, loneliness, anxiety, and social withdrawal. Friends can be there for single moms in ways that most people's families can't.

According to a 2019 study by the Pew Research Center,[7] the US has the world's highest rate of children living in single-parent households. They're also far less likely to live in extended families. When thinking about the importance of friendships between single people, we can't just focus on those that grow *before* someone falls in love, gets married, or has kids—we should also focus on the friendships people need after relationships break down and they become single again.

Being the single friend doesn't mean being the desperate friend, the party friend, or the selfish friend, just as being the friend with kids or a long-term partner shouldn't mean being reduced to domesticity, baby shower catch-ups, and dinner parties where only other couples are welcome. The joy of imagining the future of friendship comes in accepting its uncertainty—the knowledge that if none of life's guarantees are actually that, there is always a new path to tread, even if it's alongside people you might not have expected.

Long-term relationships need long-term friends

When I receive Max Dickins's out-of-office email response telling me he is on his honeymoon, I'm delighted, but not entirely surprised. After all, I'd just spent the weekend reading about his wedding plans. When we eventually meet over Zoom, Max has just returned to his home in London after ten days in Tuscany with his new wife, Naomi.

In the opening chapter of his book *Billy No-Mates: How I Realized Men Have a Friendship Problem*,[8] Max is shopping for an engagement ring for Naomi with his former housemates, Philippa and Hope. That evening, alone in his apartment, Max tries to draft a list of friends he might consider asking to be his best man, after being probed by Philippa while browsing jewelry stores. He comes up short. With ten names in front of him, Max realizes he hasn't spoken to some of these guys for years. When he checks his recent texts, Max sees he hasn't sent or received a message from a friend in two months. Somewhere between meeting Naomi and wanting to propose to her, his male friendships had all but disappeared.

Despite Max's close friendships with Hope and Philippa, the idea of not having a single male friend close enough to be seriously considered for his best man was overwhelming and, he admits, a little embarrassing. In the not-so-distant past, Max had plenty of male friends—friends made in college and through work—but at one of the most pivotal moments of his life, he looked around and realized they were no longer there.

"My journey to friendlessness was not dramatic, it was the logical endpoint of a very gentle curve," he writes. "It was feigning illness to get out of going to a party. It was turning down an invite to football because 'I've got to work this weekend.' It was bumping into an old friend and saying, 'We must have a drink—I'll text you,' knowing I wouldn't. Friendship has a rhythm and I had lost it."

When I speak to Max, I want to get his thoughts on the way long-term, mostly happy romantic relationships intersect with our friendships. While I use the phrase "mostly happy" in a nod to the fact that no relationship is perfect, Max describes these kinds of real-world relationships as "dynamic." After six years with Naomi, he's comfortable admitting that while a lot of the time—most of the time—their relationship is fantastic, there are always downs to balance the many, many ups.

Since realizing he'd let many of his closest friendships slip from his grasp, Max has given a lot of thought to what his connections with his friends, or lack thereof, can tell him about himself. On a practical level, it was easy to connect the dots and figure out why he wasn't being invited to the pub anymore, after repeatedly rejecting invitations. But to get to the heart of why he'd left many of his friendships to die on the vine, he had to dig a bit deeper. "On a more holistic level, your friendships can be reflective of where you're at emotionally," he tells me. "Like, are you self-aware? Are you investing in your emotional intelligence? Are you looking after your mental health? A lot of men don't consider self-care a big part of friendships or their romantic relationship."

A study titled "Unique ways in which the quality of friendships matter for life satisfaction"[9] investigated how friendships interact with our intimate relationships. Researchers found that when people were highly satisfied with their love life, they were generally happy, regardless of the quality of their friendships. However, if someone was unsatisfied in their romantic relationship, they only reported being happy if they had good friends. It could be easy to look at a study like this and find confirmation that, yes, love is all you need. But the expectation that relationships can be good all the time isn't just unrealistic, it's impossible.

Sometimes, when I feel like hurting my own feelings with a heavy hit of nostalgia, I'll scroll back through text message threads and email conversations I had with friends before I was in a serious relationship—when I had half the familial obligations and double the free time I do now. Almost every day for months at a time, my friend Tim and I would email each other links to Thought Catalog articles with titles like "23 Things That Will Cause a Shame Spiral In Your 20s" and subject lines like "This will be us if we ever get boyfriends!" We no longer share a constant barrage of screenshots and links and date updates with one another because we're both in long-term relationships that aren't just private but are *constant*—in a lovely, but also kind of boring way. In a mostly happy long-term relationship, it's impossible to re-create those years of stickiness where everything from boyfriends to jobs to roommates felt replaceable, but friendships never did.

Many of the topics Max explores in his book—which we cover during our call—focus on male friendships, but they're not all exclusive to straight men who have woken up one day and found themselves distanced from the people they once felt closest to. Dolly Alderton writes about similar experiences in her memoir *Everything I Know About Love*.[10] When thinking about the shift that occurs when a friend gets into a new relationship, Dolly writes that everything can change.

"These gaps in each other's lives slowly but surely form a gap in the middle of your friendship. The love is still there, but the familiarity is not," she writes. "Before you know it, you're not living life together anymore. You're living life separately with respective boyfriends, then meeting up for dinner every six weekends to tell each other what living is like." And it's not just in my imagination. Or Max's. Or Dolly's. According to research on the intersection of romance and friendship, the distance many people in relationships feel from their close friends is common.

In an interview with *The Atlantic*,[11] renowned friendship researcher Robin Dunbar—best known for his theory Dunbar's Number, that people can't have more than 150 meaningful relationships—referred to his study, which found that falling in love will cost you exactly two friendships. "If you meet a new person, fall in love, and get married, then you're investing a lot of time and mental energy in that relationship. And from our data, it seems that you essentially sacrifice two people," said Dunbar.

This concept centers on Dunbar's belief that most people's inner circle is restricted to five individuals. However, due to the closeness people feel with their lovers, along with the time, effort, and attention these relationships generally require, Dunbar believes a new relationship actually takes up two friendship "rations." Then it's a domino effect—two friends fall out from that inner circle into a wider one, pushing other people from that circle outward, and so on.

For people who like to keep their friends close, Dunbar's findings may be a bummer to hear. Nobody wants to lose a close friend—especially for the sake of a new boyfriend or girlfriend, no matter how attractive or charming they are. But this kind of friendship sacrifice can have a serious impact on the future of your relationship too. This new love who was so thrilling can slowly, over many years, become boring if you make the mistake of letting go of all the other relationships in your life.

In *Mating in Captivity: Unlocking Erotic Intelligence*,[12] every millennial woman's favorite psychotherapist, Esther Perel, says that adult intimacy has become overburdened with expectations. "Today, we turn to one person to provide what an entire village once did: a sense of grounding, meaning, and continuity," writes Perel. "At the same time, we expect our committed relationships to be romantic as well as emotionally and sexually fulfilling. Is it any wonder that so many relationships crumble under the weight of it all?"

Perel's work is so popular because it explains how long-term relationships begin to feel stale, even when they are still filled with love and emotional affection. By expecting a partner to also be a best friend, Perel believes, we're robbing them of the ability to remain mysterious and therefore desirable to us. In her writing, Perel doesn't often refer to friendship as the answer to the issues that are arising in so many modern relationships, but if our partner shouldn't be everything to us, who other than our close friends would be best placed to take on some of their duties?

At the end of *Billy No-Mates*, Max asks Philippa and Hope to lead his bridal party as joint "best women." That decision,

Max tells me, felt even more meaningful after his attempts to reconnect with some of his lost male friends. He never wanted his two friends to feel as though they were chosen because there were no other options—he wanted to choose them because they were the right people for the job. It's easier to label someone a close friend when you have other, less close but still meaningful friendships to compare them to.

Before we end our call, I ask Max if he's felt a shift in his relationship with Naomi since he started investing in his friendships more. I'm curious about the emotional impact on his relationship, now that he's spending more time with friends, dedicating more attention to them, and opening up to them about his mental health.

"Naomi is often holding me to account when it comes to my friendships. On one level, this is out of concern for my happiness. But it is also totemic: the strength of my friendships, my investment in my social world, is a microcosm of my investment in myself," he tells me. "This all rolls back around to our marriage eventually, of course. What will make you a better friend will make you a better spouse. Because if I am investing in my mental health, if I am rejuvenating myself in the healing spring of the social world, then I will be, as they say, strong enough for two."

I relate to Naomi a lot at this moment, not just because we're both women in heterosexual relationships or because we both deeply love the people we are with, but because we both clearly recognize the immeasurable value of our partner's friendships. This is why one of the things I love most about my own partner is the closeness and depth of his friendships.

I see the care my partner puts into his friendships. When I witness him keeping traditions with his friends who have been closer to him far longer than I have, I know that the traditions we have with each other will also last. When I see him reach for his phone or excuse himself to take a call from a friend—not out of obligation but pure delight—I can imagine that when it's me on the other end of the line, his face brightens just the same way. The excited inflection of the "hello mate" he reserves for his closest friends reminds me of the steadfastness of his words, his loyalty, his excitement, and his gratitude for the people who know him best. His inner circle is such a joyous place to be, I'm thankful for the fact other people are lucky enough to experience it too. His love is more real because I'm not the only one to feel it.

Friendship as a safe place

Just as it is important to recognize the joy of love and affection, it's vital we take time to sit with the hurt it can cause—specifically, the pain people we love can cause. In her memoir *In the Dream House*,[13] Carmen Maria Machado writes about the role friends can play as witnesses to domestic abuse. Friends are often the first people to notice red eyes after tense phone calls, hear excuses for bad behavior, and pay attention to bruised egos, spirits, or bodies. In the book,

Machado writes about her own experience in an abusive relationship, which is peppered with small details of the role her friends played during one of the most complex and difficult periods of her life.

"One day she asks, *Who knows about us?* It becomes a refrain. It's strange—in some past generation this could have meant so many things. Who knows we're together? Who knows we're lovers? Who knows we're queer?" writes Machado. "But when she asks, the unspoken reason is awful, deflated of nobility or romance. Who knows that I yell at you like this? Who's heard about the incident over Christmas?" While reflecting on her broken relationship, Machado shares glimpses of moments her friends witnessed, including the night she fell asleep while watching a movie with friends, only to wake to a barrage of missed calls from her former partner, who was convinced Machado was cheating on her. Sometime later, after Machado and her partner had broken up, one of these same friends stopped her from answering a call from her ex, which they both knew could easily have led to their reunion.

While the exact moments, tensions, and people Machado describes in her memoir are unique, less so is the situation she found herself in. Madison Griffiths met Theo* at a party. They had mutual friends, and unlike some people, she was drawn to his eccentricity, rather than puzzled by it. Theo was unconventional, not particularly personable, and often judgmental, constantly cycling through jobs and raising alarm bells for Madison's family. But she was enthralled.

Within three months of meeting, they were officially dating. "He had a real chip on his shoulder," Madison tells me. "He was the sort of guy who thought everyone else was wrong because he was always right. I was the opposite kind of person. I thought everyone I met had great qualities, but I was also [. . .] going through an identity crisis."

As we talk, Madison describes her relationship with Theo as a fever dream. Like many others who have endured abusive relationships, Madison felt that she was the only person who truly understood Theo, as if she were the only person who could help him. At times, it felt easy to justify his behavior—the yelling, the threats, the name-calling—by blaming his past experience with drug psychosis. Sometimes it was easy to feel as though everyone else was just being too hard on him. When Theo told Madison he was going overseas, her friends and parents begged her not to follow him—but she did.

Madison wanted to see Theo, but she too was concerned about her decision. "A few nights before I left [. . .] I sent him some messages saying, 'I'm nervous I'm going to come and you're going to, you know, *do what you do*,'" she tells me. "That was my code word for his cruel behavior." As soon as she arrived, Madison knew she'd made a mistake. Their time apart had only left Theo more emboldened than ever.

First, Madison left for a nearby country, to stay with two friends she'd met years earlier. They made space for her and cared for her. They chopped Madison's long dark hair into a bob (Theo had always hated her hair short). They insisted

Madison stay with them for Christmas. Instead, Theo called and invited her back. She wrote her friends a card and left in the middle of the night.

Before Madison had left, a different friend suggested she record the next fight she had with Theo. Their hope was that she could relisten to the argument in the sobering light of day and realize that she shouldn't be treated like this. So she did. She recorded Theo's taunts. After listening to them the following morning she called a friend, Kelly, and said she needed to get back to Australia. Kelly sent her seven hundred dollars and told her to get on the next flight home. And that's exactly what she did.

Madison tells me there was a simple reason she reached out to her friends, rather than her parents: She knew it would be easier for her friends not to judge her need for help. "They didn't have that parental feeling that they'd failed or hadn't been able to protect me from this person or that they had in some way enabled the relationship," says Madison. Her parents had tried to stop her from going by telling her they weren't going to help her fund the trip if she got in trouble. Unsure of how to handle such a distressing situation, they inadvertently made themselves off-limits in Madison's time of need. Madison tells me that she would rather have stayed overseas for another three months, waiting for the flight she had already booked to come home, than ask her parents for money.

I think about the power dynamics that can often exist between us and our parents as we reach our late teens, then our early twenties. A parent's not liking a boyfriend, a tattoo,

a haircut, or a decision to quit your job rarely feels as con-
sequential as it would if you got the same feedback from a
friend—even if the issues raised by a parent were just as valid,
if not more so. While Madison was struggling with the power
dynamics of domestic abuse, the thought of battling with her
parents was too overwhelming to even consider.

When Madison landed back in Australia, on the flight
Kelly had paid for, another friend picked her up from the
airport and took her home to offer her a shower, wash her
clothes, feed her—to mother her—until she was ready to
face her real mother.

Survivors of domestic abuse often describe a silent belief
that if they don't have their partner, they might have no
one. Madison—like many survivors, including Machado—
worked extremely hard to keep her pain contained, neatly
bundled in layers and layers of excuses and secrets to avoid
having the unsightly truth about her relationship leak out.
But whenever the truth about Theo did bleed into her life
outside her relationship, it was her friends who noticed it
seeping through a forgotten gap.

When I ask Madison about the record-keeping her friends
were doing, which enabled them to understand how to help
her as soon as she was ready, she refers to it as "the labor of
witnessing." It wasn't until she was home safely, her hair still
sitting short above her shoulders, that she was able to ask a
friend to listen to the recording of that final fight. In a second,
the truth was no longer being protected, wrapped, or stored
away—it was being shared in a moment of vulnerability

during which Madison was saying to her friend, *Don't let this happen to me again.*

According to the National Coalition Against Domestic Violence,[14] one in four women and one in nine men have experienced severe intimate partner physical violence, intimate partner sexual violence, or have been stalked by an intimate partner, resulting in such consequences as injury, fearfulness, and posttraumatic stress. When thinking about the ways our romantic relationships and friendships intersect, it feels grim to consider domestic abuse a reason to keep your most trusted friends within reach. However, isolation is a tactic used by many abusers, who work to create physical and emotional separation between their victims and their support networks. To ignore this reality would be to ignore the experiences of millions of people in this country who have survived domestic violence. And it would be to turn away from those who didn't.

From lovers to friends

There are many ways a relationship can come to an end, just as there are many ways to fall in love. Sometimes relationships end because of mistreatment, broken trust, or infidelity. People can fall out of love. People die. Regardless of how happy a relationship is in the beginning, the middle, or even at the end, it's never possible to know how something will end. Sometimes, if you're lucky, an imperfect relationship can transition into something just as worthwhile: a friendship.

When I speak to Rebecca (Bec) Shaw and Ally Garrett, they're sitting together on a couch in the apartment Ally shares with her partner. They have plans to head out together that night, and Bec's girlfriend Freya is going along too. I've intruded on their Sunday afternoon because I want to ask them about their past relationship and very present friendship.

"I thought Bec was hot, so I decided to hit on her. But unfortunately, because of who Bec is as a person, it took us a really long time to get together," Ally jokes, remembering how she and Bec started dating, years earlier. From the beginning, it was a relationship easily confused with friendship. First, by Bec who missed Ally's very obvious attraction to her and unsubtle seduction tactics. Then, by a friend of Ally's who came home to find the two watching a movie together and decided to join them for the rest of the night, completely unaware that it was, in fact, a first date she was crashing. While they were dating, Bec was in an open relationship with a different primary partner. Bec and Ally spent six months together before they felt a shift in the relationship; a little messiness with a few mistakes made on both sides, but mostly just a shared feeling that what they had was petering out. They didn't break up as much as they just went back to being friends, now with a new degree of closeness.

"Bec and I still have a lot of emotional intimacy in our friendship," Ally tells me. "Whenever I'm about to do or think something awful, Bec is who I text first. I have a lot of very close friends, but Bec is still that number one."

"I think part of us dating was that I wanted to be friends with Ally," says Bec. "We dated because we got along really well and that's also why we have a great friendship now."

I ask Bec and Ally why they think people in the queer community—Bec is a lesbian, while Ally is bisexual—seem to find it easier to be friends with their exes than most straight people I know. There are a few factors, they tell me. First, the community is a lot smaller, especially in Australian towns and cities. "If you cut out everyone in Sydney who you or your friends had had a thing with, you'd soon run out of people to be friends with," says Bec.

The second reason is that many people in the community have a more fluid approach to relationships, whether it be through ethical non-monogamy or polyamory. And while there are plenty of couples in monogamous relationships—like those that Bec and Ally are currently in with new partners—there's less likely to be judgment around the blurred lines that can make it easier to go from friends to lovers, then back again. Bec tells me that the first day her current girlfriend landed in Sydney from Aotearoa (New Zealand), they went straight to Ally's house for Christmas lunch.

"If you were to imagine that it was a straight relationship, where someone was like, 'My long-distance girlfriend is landing and we're going to my ex's for Christmas,' it would probably be a huge red flag to a straight woman," Ally tells me. But for them, it's different. What I'm most curious about when speaking to Bec and Ally is how being romantically involved has influenced the obvious closeness of their friendship.

Beyond the physical intimacy that comes with a romance, there is also a vulnerability that grows within that familiarity. When dating someone, we're more likely to open up about our past relationships and hopes for the future, and surface our deepest wounds, which may take far longer to share with a new friend. This was Bec and Ally's experience, at least.

By dating first, they were able to fast-forward their friendship to the place it is now, where they've been able to continue holding on to the best parts of their connection, while leaving other layers of intimacy behind. Without the stress of wondering "Is this going to end?" or "What are we to each other?" their friendship has been able to flourish.

During our conversation, Bec and Ally have both good and bad things to say about their experiences with non-monogamy. But the one thing that rings true for them both is the lesson these kinds of relationships teach you about love: that you can't expect one person to fulfill all of your needs. In non-monogamous relationships, these other needs are filled by different partners, dates, and hook-ups. But for people like Ally and Bec, who can recognize this value while still wanting to be in an exclusive, monogamous relationship, it's now about considering how friends can fill the spaces in your life that no single partner would ever be able to do.

In many straight—and some queer—relationships, a lack of trust is what prevents people from being friends with former lovers or becoming friends with people they may also be attracted to. Of course, trust is the foundation of every healthy relationship. There's the trust that someone won't leave you, even if they talk to or spend time with someone they could also be sexually attracted to. But the trust that is just as important is the kind that allows your partner to fill their life with as many smart, funny, interesting, caring, and good-looking people as they wish, without jeopardizing your closeness at all. To me, that kind of trust is the real hallmark of success.

A contract for friendship

In *Boy Friends*, Michael Pedersen considers the need for a contract for friendship. We have contracts for marriages and employment, he points out, why not for our friendships too?

Despite my love of the frivolity and festivity of weddings, I've had trouble seeing the true value of marriage for myself. It's something I've spoken at length about with my partner, my friends, and my family. So why did I find this idea of a friendship contract so intriguing? Why, when I can find such comfort, commitment and happiness in my own relationship, without the need for a traditional ceremony and marriage certificate, would I ever wish to apply that same formality to my friendships? After all, isn't the fact that we aren't tempted to bind friendships in contracts part of what makes them special?

To me, declarations and celebrations of friendship, like Nerida's and Maddi's, feel deeply symbolic. In them, I see a sign of changing tides when it comes to the hierarchy of love. But a contract will never be a real replacement for commitment—not in friendship or romantic love. At least, the act of marriage will never replace the kind of emotional commitment truly required to keep loving someone, caring for them, and letting them really see you for the rest of your life.

Instead of a friendship contract, perhaps the only way to really build an equilibrium between our lovers and friends is to treat the former more like the latter, not the other way around. In a world where marriage didn't exist—or at least wasn't the measure of personal and societal success it is today—perhaps we could view our romances more like we do our closest friendships: as relationships that are not governed or guaranteed by the very act of signing your names alongside witnesses, but as relationships that will be as long and strong as the continual effort you put into them. Valuing romantic partnerships above all else hasn't stopped the need for divorce or saved millions of people from heartbreak, and yet society remains committed to the idea that romantic love is always the answer. Why?

I've come to realize that the belief that marriage is a promise of stability leads us to assume romantic relationships can be effortless. But to me, this idea only distracts from the consistent effort my partner and I put into our love and the dedication it requires to keep loving someone for who they are, as well as who they are becoming. I believe people can be a close-to-perfect match (my partner and I included), but I also believe the stories we tell ourselves about romantic love are holding us back. If soulmates really do exist, who's to say they can't be a friend?

Conclusion: A Promise

It's amazing what can happen in a year.

Pleasant surprises, disappointments, and decisions can change everything. People leave, while others come home. You can miss out on things you really wanted but be gifted moments you didn't realize you needed. Entire books can be written. Perspectives can be changed.

When I started writing this book, I already considered myself to be a good friend. I cared, I cooked, I showed up. When I told people about the book's topic, there were no looks of surprise or confusion, only affirming nods and encouraging words, which reminded me that my decision to dive heart first toward friendship made sense. At that time, I knew there was more to learn about the power of friendship, in all its iterations, but looking back, I can see I underestimated just how much.

The Saturday night after I wrote about the liking gap, I decided to go to a birthday party I'd planned on skipping. I spoke to people I'd only met once or twice, and many others I was meeting for the first time. I pushed myself through crowds and conversations with the knowledge that I was most likely underestimating how much people at the party liked me. The change I felt within myself that night was dizzying.

After coming across a study titled "I like that you feel my pain, but I love that you feel my joy,"[1] which found that we want those closest to us to celebrate our wins just as much as they comfort us through our hurt, I tried to do just that. I've always prided myself on being a good listener, someone to turn to on the worst day, who will make up a bed in the spare room, do your grocery shopping, and maybe give you advice, if you're up for it. But I'd never considered the importance of putting in that same level of effort for people who have just *done the thing*. After learning that flowers and kind texts and tight hugs can be just as meaningful when reacting to the good things in life as to the bad, I felt my own focus shift. I saw how much it meant to people. I took note when friends returned with more good news, after being reminded how excited I was to celebrate them. The closer I came to writing this final chapter, the more important it felt to ask myself: What would it look like, in practice, to take more of my own advice when it comes to friendship?

What I've learned is that it looks like a lot of tiny things. It's listening to tipsy friends when they tell me they don't know what they'd do without me and believing that it's true.

It's taking the obligation I feel toward my family and applying that same dedication to my friendships. It's pressing pause on life—even in the most inconvenient moments—and being there for the people I would want to do the same for me. It's remembering that no matter how many times I've done all of these things in the past, the most important thing is to continue them into the future.

One year on, the art of practicing what you preach has never felt so within my grasp.

When imagining what this book might become, I hoped to understand how my own friends came to mean so much to me; I wanted an answer to the question, a formula on how to ensure that these relationships go from strength to strength. But the truth is, there is no end to the work that needs to be done if there is ever to be a real shift when it comes to realigning the importance of our relationships. For friendships to no longer sit in the shadows of everything we've been taught to believe about nuclear families and soulmates, we need to keep talking, keep searching, and keep trying.

This book is not an end point, but a starting point. It's a reminder that no matter how passionately you adore your friends or how clearly you see their worth, there is always further to stretch. There are always more promises to make. Even if you already love your friends fiercely, there is always more room to grow.

You don't have to have a lifelong best friend to be someone who cares about friendship. You don't even have to feel like you have any close friends at all. In every conversation

I had while writing, even when talking to people about the friends they loved most, or had lost forever, flaws almost always emerged. There are endless opportunities for people to show up or let you down, and for you to do both of those things in return, but committing to friendship means understanding that even our most important relationships aren't without their imperfections.

I wasn't drawn to this work because I consider myself a perfect friend, but I hope to be a better friend now that I have done the thinking, listening, and reflecting necessary to push back on what society expects us to believe about the value of friendship. Because caring deeply about friendship isn't just about the individuals who make up our treasured relationships; it's also about challenging the forces that ask us to place these people second. To give friendship the power it deserves, we need to adjust the scales that prioritize our productivity, our families, and our partners above all else.

All of us, whether we're aware of it or not, have fallen into the habit of putting our friendships second. The label "just friends," which so many of us use in an offhand way, exists as a counterpoint to "lovers." It is a way to minimize our friendships so they don't become something our romantic partners need to fear or envy. But with all I know about love and about friendship, I can see that "just" exists only to downplay the relationships that, for many people, end up mattering the most.

Who is there to make us feel at home in new neighborhoods and countries? Who provides comfort at work and safety outside our relationships? Who do we go to when our hearts get broken? And who makes being alone by society's current standards feel anything but lonely? More than ever, I am firm in the belief that the only answer to all of these questions is our friends. And it's about time we put them first.

Notes

Introduction

1. L. C. Giles, "Effect of social networks on 10 year survival in very old Australians: The Australian longitudinal study of aging," *Journal of Epidemiology & Community Health* 59, no. 7 (2005): 574–79.
2. Hailing Zhang et al., "Experiences of Social Support Among Chinese Women with Breast Cancer: A Qualitative Analysis Using a Framework Approach," *Medical Science Monitor* 24 (January 2018): 574–81.

1. Meet Cute

1. Sable Yong, "The Ex-Girlfriend Experience," Hard Feelings, February 14, 2023, hardfeelings.substack.com/p/the-ex-girlfriend-experience.
2. Aminatou Sow and Ann Friedman, *Big Friendship: How We Keep Each Other Close* (New York: Simon & Schuster, 2020), xv.
3. Rachel Wilkerson Miller, *The Art of Showing Up: How to Be There for Yourself and Your People* (New York: The Experiment, 2020), 146.
4. Gillian M. Sandstrom and Elizabeth W. Dunn, "Social Interactions and Well-Being: The Surprising Power of Weak Ties," *Personality and Social Psychology Bulletin* 40, no. 7 (2014): 910–22.
5. Ingrid Culos et al., "Foundations for Belonging: A snapshot of newly arrived refugees," Settlement Services International Western Sydney University Institute for Culture and Society (2020), ssi.org.au/wp-content/uploads/2023/05/Foundations-for-Belonging-A-snapshot-of-newly-arrived-refugees.pdf.

6. Jeffrey A. Hall, "How many hours does it take to make a friend?," *Journal of Social and Personal Relationships* 36, no. 4 (2018): 1278–96.

7. Stephanie Convery and Luke Henriques-Gomes, "Women do 21 hours more unpaid work than men a week, national survey finds," *The Guardian*, December 6, 2021, theguardian.com/australia-news/2021/dec/07/women-do-21-hours-more-unpaid-work-than-men-study-suggests.

8. Peggy J. Liu et al. "The surprise of reaching out: Appreciated more than we think," *Journal of Personality and Social Psychology* 124, no. 4 (2023): 754–71.

9. Nicholas Epley, *Mindwise: How We Understand What Others Think, Believe, Feel, and Want* (New York: Knopf, 2014).

10. Marisa G. Franco, *Platonic: How the Science of Attachment Can Help You Make—and Keep—Friends* (New York: G. P. Putnam's Sons, 2022).

11. Jeremy Dean, "The Acceptance Prophecy: How You Control Who Likes You," PsyBlog, August 27, 2009, spring.org.uk/2009/08/the-acceptance-prophesy-how-you-control-who-likes-you.php.

12. Sylvia A. Morelli et al., "Empathy and well-being correlate with centrality in different social networks," *Proceedings of the National Academy of Sciences* 114, no. 37 (2017): 9843–47.

13. Ray Oldenburg, *The Great Good Place* (New York: Paragon House, 1989).

14. Vincent A. Landau et al., "Analysis of the Disparities in Nature Loss and Access to Nature," Conservation Science Partners, May 29, 2020, csp-inc.org/public/CSP-CAP_Disparities_in_Nature_Loss_FINAL_Report_060120.pdf.

2. The Friendship Recipe

1. Julie Beck, "The Six Forces That Fuel Friendship," *The Atlantic*, June 10, 2022.

2. Haley Nahman, "#120: Living 'aesthetically,' friend-group envy, and a new climate doom approach," October 20, 2022, haleynahman.substack.com/p/120-living-aesthetically-friend-group.

3. Chelsea Fagan (@Chelsea_Fagan), Twitter/X post, September 16, 2022, twitter.com/Chelsea_Fagan/status/1570856733010186240.

4. Priya Parker, *The Art of Gathering: How We Meet and Why It Matters* (New York: Riverhead Books, 2018), 71, 74, 92.

3. Family Matters

1. William J. Chopik, "Associations among relational values, support, health, and well-being across the adult lifespan," *Personal Relationships* 24 (2017): 408–22.

2. "No. HS-12, Households by Type and Size: 1900 to 2002," U.S. Census Bureau, Statistical Abstract of the United States: 2003, www2.census.gov/library/publications/2004/compendia/statab/123ed/hist/hs-12.pdf. Accessed January 20, 2024.

3. Jesper Rözer et al., "Family and Friends: Which Types of Personal Relationships Go Together in a Network?" *Social Indicators Research* 127, no. 2 (2015): 809–26.

4. Andrew Solomon, *Far from the Tree: A Dozen Kinds of Love* (New York: Scribner, 2012), 20.

5. Kim Parker and Eileen Patten, "The Sandwich Generation: Rising Financial Burdens for Middle-Aged Americans," Pew Research Center, January 30, 2013, pewresearch.org/social-trends/2013/01/30/the-sandwich-generation.

6. Vera L. Buijs et al., "Interdependencies between family and friends in daily life: Personality differences and associations with affective well-being across the lifespan," *European Journal of Personality* 37, no. 2 (2022): 154–70.

4. It Takes a Village

1. David Brooks, "The Nuclear Family Was a Mistake," *The Atlantic*, February 10, 2020.

2. Minna Salami, "The Western concept of family needs to move with the times," CNN Style, March 8, 2019, edition.cnn.com/style/article/minna-salami-family/index.html.

3. Andrea Reupert et al., "It Takes a Village to Raise a Child: Understanding and Expanding the Concept of the 'Village,'" *Frontiers in Public Health* (March 11, 2022).

4. Bonnie Angelo and Toni Morrison, "Toni Morrison: The Pain of Being Black," *Time*, May 22, 1989.

5. Hannah McElhinney, *Rainbow History Class: Your Guide Through Queer and Trans History* (Melbourne, VIC: Hardie Grant Books, 2023).

6. Kath Weston, *Families We Choose: Lesbians, Gays, Kinship* (New York: Columbia University Press, 1991).

7. Steven Canals et al., *Pose*, season 1, episode 8, "Mother of the Year," aired July 22, 2018, FX.

8. Marlon M. Bailey, *Butch Queens Up in Pumps: Gender, Performance, and Ballroom Culture in Detroit* (Ann Arbor: University of Michigan Press, 2013).

9. Marlon M. Bailey, "Structures of kinship in Ballroom culture," *Architectural Review*, March 16, 2021, architectural-review.com/essays/gender-and-sexuality/structures-of-kinship-in-ballroom-culture.

10. Larry Thompson, "Widening AZT use may drain blood supply," *The Washington Post*, April 21, 1987.

11. Beth Hutchison, "Lesbian Blood Drives as Community-Building Activism in the 1980s," *Journal of Lesbian Studies* 19, no. 1 (2015): 117–28.

12. Joy Harden Bradford, *Sisterhood Heals: The Transformative Power of Healing in Community* (New York: Ballantine Books, 2023).

5. The Care Factor

1. Gyan Yankovich, "Unconventional Life Hack: Always Offer to Help Your Friends Move," Man Repeller, July 23, 2019.

2. bell hooks, *All About Love: New Visions* (New York: William Morrow Paperbacks, 2018), 4, 6, 13, 54.

3. Gary D. Chapman, *The Five Love Languages: How to Express Heartfelt Commitment to Your Mate* (Chicago: Northfield Publishing, 1992).

4. Cathryn Lavery (@cathrynlavery), Twitter/X post, January 15, 2023, twitter.com/cathrynlavery/status/1614668597166747649?lang=en.

5. Katy Waldman, "'The Rise of Therapy-Speak," *The New Yorker*, March 26, 2021.

6. Melissa A. Fabello (@fyeahmfabello), Twitter/X post, November 18, 2019, twitter.com/fyeahmfabello/status/1196581296564256768.

7. Susan Silk and Barry Goldman, "How not to say the wrong thing," *Los Angeles Times*, April 7, 2013.

8. Shelley E. Taylor, "Tend and Befriend Theory," in A. M. van Lange et al. (ed.), *Handbook of Theories of Social Psychology* (Thousand Oaks, CA: Sage Publications, 2011).

9. Brooke McAlary, *Care: The Radical Art of Taking Time* (Crows Nest, NSW: Allen & Unwin, 2021), 11, 12, 14.

10. Audre Lorde, *A Burst of Light: Essays* (Ithaca, NY: Firebrand Books, 1988).

6. In the Group Chat

1. Riley A. Scott et al., "Connecting with Close Friends Online: A qualitative analysis of young adults' perceptions of online and offline social interactions with friends," *Computers in Human Behavior Reports* 7 (August 2022).

2. Henri Tajfel, "The Achievement of Inter-group Differentiation," *Differentiation Between Social Groups: Studies in the Social Psychology of Intergroup Relations* (London: Academic Press, 1978), 77–100.

3. Isabella Kwai, "How 'Subtle Asian Traits' Became a Global Hit," *The New York Times*, December 11, 2018.

4. Jia Tolentino, *Trick Mirror: Reflections on Self-Delusion* (New York: Random House, 2019), 7, 8.

5. Sheila Liming, *Hanging Out: The Radical Power of Killing Time* (Brooklyn, NY: Melville House, 2023), 8, 9.

6. Daniel Kahneman, *Thinking, Fast and Slow* (New York: Farrar, Straus and Giroux, 2011).

7. Kristen S. He, "MUNA's New Album Is Joy as an Act of Resistance," Junkee, August 31, 2022, junkee.com munas-self-titled-album-profile/340106.

8. Joe Hunting, *We Met in Virtual Reality*, HBO, 2022.

9. Gabrielle Zevin, *Tomorrow, and Tomorrow, and Tomorrow* (New York: Vintage, 2022), 21.

7. Working It Out

1. Jaime Green, "Bodega Beans Are the Best Thing to Eat When You're Broke," BuzzFeed News, January 22, 2019, buzzfeednews.com/article/jaimegreen/bodega-beans-broke-credit-card-debt-area-of-expertise.

2. Adam Roberts, "Rachel Wharton's Bodega Beans," The Amateur Gourmet, December 13, 2007, amateurgourmet.com/2007/12/rachel_whartons.html.

3. Sheryl Sandberg, *Lean In: Women, Work, and the Will to Lead* (New York: Alfred A. Knopf, 2013).

4. Arianne Cohen, "How to Quit Your Job in the Great Post-Pandemic Resignation Boom," Bloomberg, May 10, 2021, bloomberg.com/news/articles/2021-05-10/quit-your-job-how-to-resign-after-covid-pandemic.

5. Joseph Fuller and William Kerr, "The Great Resignation Didn't Start with the Pandemic," *Harvard Business Review*, March 23, 2022, hbr.org/2022/03/the-great-resignation-didnt-start-with-the-pandemic.

6. Noreena Hertz, *The Lonely Century: A Call to Reconnect* (New York: Currency, 2021).

7. "Open Office Floor Plan Research Study: Trends and Insights on the Future of the Open Office Floor Plan," Stegmeier Consulting Group, stegmeierconsulting.com/research/state-of-the-open-office-research-study.

8. Anne Helen Petersen, *Can't Even: How Millennials Became the Burnout Generation* (New York: Vintage, 2021), xxii, 68, 70.

9. Anne Helen Petersen, "How Millennials Became the Burnout Generation," BuzzFeed News, January 5, 2019, buzzfeednews.com/article/annehelenpetersen/millennials-burnout-generation-debt-work.

10. Sarah Jaffe, *Work Won't Love You Back: How Devotion to Our Jobs Keeps Us Exploited, Exhausted, and Alone* (New York: Bold Type Books, 2021).

11. Elizabeth Rivelli, "How Much Does It Cost to Have a Baby? 2024 Averages," *Forbes*, October 10, 2022, forbes.com/advisor/health-insurance/average-childbirth-cost.

12. Anna Patty, "The family-friendly work illusion turning women off having children," *Sydney Morning Herald*, October 28, 2019.

13. Elizabeth Hill et al., "Young women and men: Imagined futures of work and family formation in Australia," *Journal of Sociology* 55, no. 4 (2019): 778–98.

14. Ashley Stahl, "New Study: Millennial Women Are Delaying Having Children Due to Their Careers," *Forbes*, May 1, 2020, forbes.com/sites/ashleystahl/2020/05/01/new-study-millennial-women-are-delaying-having-children-due-to-their-careers/?sh=76d51ad3276a.

15. Erica Cerulo and Claire Mazur, *Work Wife: The Power of Female Friendship to Drive Successful Businesses* (New York: Ballantine Books, 2019), 88.

16. Tilly Lawless, *Nothing But My Body* (Crows Nest, NSW: Allen & Unwin, 2021).

8. Breakups and Breakdowns

1. Patti Miller, *True Friends* (St. Lucia, QLD: University of Queensland Press, 2022), 100, 273.

2. Cheryl Harasymchuk and Beverley Fehr, "Responses to dissatisfaction in friendships and romantic relationships: An interpersonal script analysis," *Journal of Social and Personal Relationships* 36, no. 6 (2018): 1651–70.

3. Carly Breit, "Why Ending a Friendship Can Be Worse than a Breakup," *Time*, September 24, 2018.

4. Marni Feuerman, *Ghosted and Breadcrumbed: Stop Falling for Unavailable Men and Get Smart About Healthy Relationships* (Novato, CA: New World Library, 2019).

5. C. S. Lewis, *The Four Loves* (San Francisco: HarperOne, 1960), 98.

6. Hannah Korrel, *How to Break Up with Friends: From Friendsh*t to Friendsplit: A Guide to Ditching Crappy Companions* (Cammeray, NSW: Simon & Schuster, 2020).

7. Julianne Holt-Lunstad and Benjamin D. Clark, "Social stressors and cardiovascular response: Influence of ambivalent relationships and behavioral ambivalence," *International Journal of Psychophysiology* 93, no. 3 (2014): 381–89.

8. William J. Chopik, "Associations among relational values, support, health, and well-being across the adult lifespan," *Personal Relationships* 24, no. 2 (2017): 408–22.

9. Loved and Lost

1. Wai-Man Liu et al., "Death of a close friend: Short and long-term impacts on physical, psychological and social well-being," *PLOS ONE* 14, no. 4 (April 2019).

2. "Leading Causes of Death and Injury," Centers for Disease Control and Prevention, 2021, cdc.gov/injury/wisqars/leadingcauses.html.

3. Lech Blaine, *Car Crash: A Memoir* (Collingwood, VIC: Black Inc. Books, 2021), 36.

4. Michael Pedersen, *Boy Friends* (London: Faber, 2022), 1, 140.

5. Dennis Klass et al., *Continuing Bonds: New Understandings of Grief* (Philadelphia: Taylor & Francis, 1996), 29.

6. Jonathan Tjarks, "Does My Son Know You? Fatherhood, Cancer, and What Matters Most," The Ringer, March 3, 2022, theringer.com/2022/3/3/22956353/fatherhood-cancer-jonathan-tjarks.

10. Letting Go of the One

1. Eli J. Finkel, *The All-or-Nothing Marriage: How the Best Marriages Work* (New York: Dutton, 2017).

2. Marisa G. Franco, *Platonic: How the Science of Attachment Can Help You Make—and Keep—Friends* (New York: G. P. Putnam's Sons, 2022), 241, 242.

3. Angela Chen, *Ace: What Asexuality Reveals About Desire, Society, and the Meaning of Sex* (Boston: Beacon Press, 2021).

4. Rebecca Traister, *All the Single Ladies: Unmarried Women and the Rise of an Independent Nation* (New York: Simon & Schuster, 2016), 9, 97, 108.

5. *Sex and the City*, season 6, episode 9, "A Woman's Right to Shoes," aired August 17, 2003, HBO.

6. Xiang Zhou and Zoe E. Taylor, "Differentiating the impact of family and friend social support for single mothers on parenting and internalizing symptoms," *Journal of Affective Disorders Reports* 8 (April 2022): 100319.

7. Stephanie Kramer, "U.S. has world's highest rate of children living in single-parent households," Pew Research Center, December 12, 2019, pewresearch.org/short-reads/2019/12/12/u-s-children-more-likely-than-children-in-other-countries-to-live-with-just-one-parent.

8. Max Dickins, *Billy No-Mates: How I Realised Men Have a Friendship Problem* (London: Canongate Books, 2022), 13.

9. Victor Kaufman et al., "Unique Ways in Which the Quality of Friendships Matter for Life Satisfaction," *Journal of Happiness Studies* 23 (March 2022): 2563–80.

10. Dolly Alderton, *Everything I Know About Love* (New York: Harper Perennial, 2021), 135.

11. Sheon Han, "You Can Only Maintain so Many Close Friendships," *The Atlantic*, May 20, 2021.

12. Esther Perel, *Mating in Captivity: Unlocking Erotic Intelligence* (New York: Harper, 2006), xiv, 9.

13. Carmen Maria Machado, *In the Dream House* (Minneapolis, MN: Graywolf Press, 2019), 152.

14. "Statistics," National Coalition Against Domestic Violence, ncadv.org/statistics.

Conclusion: A Promise

1. "I like that you feel my pain, but I love that you feel my joy: Empathy for a partner's negative versus positive emotions independently affect relationship quality," *Journal of Social and Personal Relationships* 36, no. 3 (2017): 834–54.

Acknowledgments

When I pick up a book, I often turn straight to the acknowledgments before I start the first chapter. There's always been something special about these pages—a peek behind the curtain, which reveals all the people who made it possible. This book in particular has been a manifestation of friendship, not only in topic but also in how it came to be.

First, to my agent, Rach Crawford, thank you for seeing what I hoped to achieve with this book, often more clearly than I could.

To my editor, Batya Rosenblum, thank you for your vision and for being a joy to work with. And to the team at The Experiment: Matthew Lore, Besse Lynch, Zach Pace, Ann J. Kirschner, and Juli Barbato.

Gina Rushton, this book wouldn't exist without you. Thank you for celebrating every interview, chapter and tiny win as if they were your own. Jenna Whyte, thank you for being my cheerleader, confidante, and the most joyful person to walk laps of Sydney Park with. Bess Murphy, thank you for a friendship that feels like home. Julia Naughton, thank you for always being a voice of reason. Tim Bussink, my oldest and most loyal friend. Who would I be without you?

Thank you to my wildly generous and intelligent friends who gave feedback on my early chapters: Haley Nahman, Mallory Rice, Lane Sainty, and Rob Stott. This book is so much better because of you.

To Mum, everything I have been lucky enough to do and achieve is all thanks to you. To my sister, Yasmin, thank you for your constant reassurance and love. And to Remy, Yuri, and Tommy, I love you all to bits. To Dad, thank you for making me feel like I can do anything I put my mind to. And to Doreen and Rob Conroy, thank you for your care and encouragement. Thank you to sweet Paddington, the perfect writing companion.

To the people who remind me every day why friendship matters so much: Jessica Bailey, Blaze Coops, Kate Holden, Louise Khong, Leda Ross, Erin Van Der Meer, Dani Pinkus, Sarah Macrae, Rachel Wilkerson Miller, Kiyana Salkeld, Terri Pous, Tom Vellner, Nikitah Habraken, Mark Scott, and many more. What did I do to deserve you all?

A heartfelt thank-you to every person who trusted me with their story, I hope I have done you and your friendships justice.

And finally, to Michael Conroy, whom I will never be able to thank enough. You are impossibly kind, patient, and thoughtful. Every day with you is better than the last. I love you.

About the Author

GYAN YANKOVICH has spent the last twelve years helping women better their relationships with themselves, the world, and the people around them. She has worked as a senior lifestyle editor at BuzzFeed and managing editor at Man Repeller and has written for The Cut, Vox, Refinery29, VICE, BuzzFeed, Man Repeller, *The Sydney Morning Herald*, PopSugar, *SELF*, *Cosmopolitan*, *InStyle*, and more. She is the lifestyle editor of two of Australia's leading newspapers, *The Sydney Morning Herald* and *The Age*, and currently lives in Sydney.

gyanyankovich.com | ⓘ gyanyankovich